# She Flies
## *Through*
# The Air

# She Flies *Through* The Air

## Circus Life

Lee Stath (Marilees)

Library of Congress Control Number:    2013919191
ISBN:          Hardcover              978-1-4931-2018-5
               Softcover              978-1-4931-2017-8
               eBook                  978-1-4931-2019-2

This book was printed in the United States of America.

Rev. date: 10/29/2013

**To order additional copies of this book, contact:**
Xlibris LLC
1-888-795-4274
www.Xlibris.com
Orders@Xlibris.com
140759

# Contents

*She Flies through the Air (Final Cut) Oct. 1, 2013*

## Chapter I

# And God Made Mary

August 23, 2006

1958, CIRCUS BOSWELL: Somewhere in the Kalahari Desert

Sundays, our day of rest. No performances were allowed in this predominately Boer part of South Africa. So, the circus used the idle time to move the show long distances to the next show grounds. This always meant eighteen to twenty-four hours on a long, long train with fifty artists; two hundred working boys; a menagerie of wild animals, horses, elephants, exotics, and the tons of circus equipment, such as tent canvas, poles, stakes, seating, dressing rooms, ticket wagons, tractors, trucks, and WC (donnikers). It was a small town moving to greener pastures. Our domicile was one cabin with four berths, two windows, and a washbasin, our home for fifty-two weeks. Bottom bunks were for sitting, eating, reading, entertaining, and sleeping. Top bunks were converted into wardrobe, and one corner held our tiny gas fridge. However, down the narrow passageway to the end of the coach, just outside the community toilet, was a small shelf that we had commandeered and held our primitive, primus cooking stove, one small burner filled with alcohol and pumped with air for a fine, hot blue flame. Many an exotic meal was created in those confines. But what to do on a Sunday afternoon? I don't recall if TV existed fifty years ago in Africa but certainly not on the old narrow gauge railway on which we traveled. Even radio was limited to the life of our wee batteries, but we did talk. Each car had ten cabins with a family or an act jungled up together. We filled the passageway, looking out of the windows as the vast, wild, desolate, arid, mountainous, exotic jungle

vista of Africa slid past. God, what joyous days. Then there were the slow stretches. The time when the steam engines would slow and struggle up a steep, long grade. But it was Sunday, and there was no show today. We were young, healthy, and there was fun to be had. That meant leaning off the coaches' platform, stepping off the stairs, and running alongside the laboring train. A few hundred feet and back aboard or pick up the pace and catch the next

"Mary, bikini clad, in a far away land."

car ahead. Young, lithe, sweaty bodies. What a treat when the fatigued, thirsty engine crawled to a stop at one of the desolate watering stops. That was when everyone—acrobat, lion tamer, juggler, and musician—stripped down and got under the huge water tower to splash, bathe, and cool under the heavy gush of tepid water. It was just one of those

LEE STATH (MARILEES)

stops—we were wearing our bathing suits and Mary had on a wee bikini.

Visualize Mary in a wee bikini. With long blonde hair, she was brown from the African sun, a body sculpted from thirty years of trapeze and a face of Germanic beauty that is unparalleled. She took offense to being compared with Marilyn Monroe. There was much more character in Mary's face: high cheekbones; brilliant, wide-set green eyes; more like Jackie O. And if I sought to compare her with any well-known beauty, perhaps Marlene Dietrich was a close second.

So there we were, clean, wet, glistening in the African sun in the middle of the Kalahari Desert. The train began to move off, no "all aboard" or any of that city stuff, just time to go and moving on. I didn't want to get sweaty, so I swung on the hand rail and up the steps. I looked back and saw Mary at a full run, fifty meters back. How were we to know they had switched from steam engine to two powerful diesel locomotives for the long haul ahead?

"Long, long circus train makes a long, long jump."

We were gathering speed fast; and the half-dozen wires, used for signaling and switching tracks, were lying a foot above the ground, running parallel to the tracks. They formed a snare between her and our coach. I motioned her back—cried out for her not to try it. But she was already out of earshot, and in a moment, we were gone.

Circus owners are businessmen and have learned ways to prosper, save, cut corners, and conserve their investments. The circus train had forty-eight cars: the wild animal cages, elephant wagons, rigging on flatcars, tractors, trucks, and our half-dozen living cars at the rear. The thought of working my way forward, over those forty-eight individual obstacles to the engineer was out of the question. Only wait till the next stop and then go looking for a bikini-clad blonde somewhere in the Kalahari Desert.

It couldn't have been more than forty-five minutes when we slowed and pulled into some small dorp. As one, we went about our allotted duties. I sent Roger up forward to hold the engineer, while four of the native boys helped me lift out the motorcycle we carried along for shopping and sightseeing. No sooner had I kick-started it into life than this dusty, dented, unpainted pickup drove up alongside; and a hard-faced, old Boer farmer got out and opened the door for Mary. She stepped out, cool and casual, kissed him on the cheek, and walked right past me, pausing only long enough to hiss, "You-son-of-a-bitch." Then she climbed on board. I rode up and told the engineer everything was OK, reloaded the cycle, and returned to our compartment where we didn't speak for a week. But, that often happened.

# Chapter II

# You Can Never Go Home

THAT WAS OVER fifty years ago. Now Mary has finally left me. After so many years of our intimate bond—an unbreakable bond, I believed—I'm not certain when she left me, though I can name it by the day, the color of the sky, the exact hour, and even the early taste of autumn. But being so close for so long, I buried myself into our togetherness. It took me weeks—no, it was months—before the realization that Mary was gone became a reality. Hadn't we survived so many turbulent times together yet each dawn found us clinging desperately to each other, promising to stay as one, promising to care for each other to the end?

But the end came early, yet the end came slowly. The first hint I had of your infidelity was during our last "hurrah," that last trip, our return to your beloved Spain. I made an elaborate itinerary, touching all your favorite places. For the first time, expense was not a consideration. We would sit in the same cafes, visit the familiar cathedrals, eat in the most expensive restaurants, and sleep in luxury, a well-deserved reward for all those years of physical abuse. We earned it. You earned it.

# Chapter III

# Life before Mary

BACK IN 1945, just after the war was over, I got a two-week leave. To spend as much time at home as possible, I put on my combat ribbons; caught a ride out to the air force base, near Los Angeles; and went looking for a plane to San Antonio. It wasn't more than an hour when a sergeant said he had a B-26 going to Tulsa. I grabbed a parachute and climbed on board. Out of Tulsa, I caught a B-25 to Detroit. I sat for ten hours in some barracks before flight on another bomber took me to down to Mobile then to Dallas; and, after two days, I arrived in San Antonio. As for the flying itself, it was not first class. Near the tail section, I found a flat metal space that allowed me to lie down. In this tube-like structure, I could identify easily with the environment of my submarine. So sleep came easily. While dozing in this noisy, flimsy bomber under untroubled, peaceful skies, I could not help but wonder what the men felt in these same aircraft, flying over enemy territory with search lights, antiaircraft bursts shattering the sky while confronting enemy fighters zooming in, around, and above, all intent on destroying your plane and all on board. With all the dangers flung by nature and pure chance, what were the terrors experienced by those men under enemy fire?

And then to return a second time, a third, and on and on, seemingly without end, until, suddenly, there was an end.

Oddly, I couldn't relate those circumstances to my war under water. At times, I felt almost cowardly, cringing against the solid, cold steel bulkheads of a submarine, hidden deep from the enemy; unseen; and, hopefully, unknown. Surface was no place for a three-hundred-foot diesel submarine. In fact, the major danger of the countless depth charges they dropped was not in the unlikely chance of a direct hit but in the surge and power they exerted when they exploded under your boat and forced the sub to the surface where you then became the proverbial "sitting duck." Or worse, still, was while trying, to escape, and the charges detonated above and the explosion would send tons of water pressure forcing the boat deeper in an accelerating dive until crush depth was achieved and the sub imploded.

Our skipper was war knowledgeable, and after our initial crash dive, he would level off and get us down slowly for a safer depth. Still, I could only sympathize for those massive, floating ships lying on the surface, carrying a thousand souls, exposed to whatever the enemy could bring to bear. I've always felt a great pride,

"SS Silversides finishes another successful war patrol."

being a select member in the "Silent Service." And "select"

it was. After volunteering, I was naïve in thinking I had been accepted. The physical was tough (claustrophobia, body odor, antagonistic personality you need not apply). You would be sleeping, cheek to jowl, with eighty-five other guys. So, for openers, I met the first of the three psychiatrists to whom I would reveal my soul before proving myself worthy of a berth aboard a fighting submarine.

Being the new man on board, I expected nothing better than the third tier of bunks, wedged between the six torpedoes lashed to the racks in the forward torpedo room. Seventeen years old and I was a torpedo man third class, going to war. I'll only comment on the positive parts of that period. We were members of a select fighting force, making up only 2 percent of the entire US Navy. Yet, at war's end, we were credited at having sunk 72 percent of all Japanese naval craft lost in that conflict. Small wonder, we garnished 50 percent extra pay for hazardous duty. We were spoiled, being served the finest food available and obtainable at any time, day or night. (Was there any difference?)

I chuckle, still, at the initiation given by the old salts, the veterans of many dives and war patrols. On my first deep dive, the chief of the boat called me to the maneuvering room, where he stretched a cord from one bulkhead to the other, saying, "Watch this, kid." "Yes, sir," I replied, though I could not recall anything similar during training. We continued the dive in routine fashion. I saw the bow and stern plane bubbles, on the instrument panel, slip to an acute angle and glanced at the depth gauge reading 150 feet. Slade Cutter, our captain of heroic dimensions with a truly heroic name, caught my eye; and a sly smile eased over his unshaven face as he turned to continue his supervision of this deep

LEE STATH (MARILEES)

dive. Now, I saw the depth gauge registering 225 feet and I heard the first faint groans of shrinking metal, sounds I would learn to live with and wonder if and when those moans and creaks would change to a full-throated scream of imploding steel. We were still descending, sinking now to 400 feet when the captain instructed to blow bow buoyancy, level off at 500 feet, and check the boat for leaks. "Well, Skeeter (that was the name they had given me after seeing the tattoo on my private parts), how's the string?" "Fine, sir," I replied reflexively, having forgotten my assignment as "string watcher"; but when I did the inevitable double take and saw the previously taut string now hanging like limp linguine, the chief and crew fell about laughing at my astonishment and wonder at the shrinking hull under this crushing weight. Even the stern captain revealed some amusement at this initiation of his newest family member. I was sincerely awestruck, but this only strengthened my confidence and respect for the old diesel, US submarines.

Then there were other rewards. When we finished a lengthy, war patrol and came back into Pearl Harbor for a refit, the crew was sent over to the famous Royal Hawaiian Hotel, now the exclusive rest and relaxation home for the submarine service. The much publicized Waikiki Beach was a bit of a disappointment with nothing but gravel and rocks. But putting on my dress whites and going into town was as exciting as my first dive, I must tell of one more of the many perks of being in the "Silent Service." Whenever we went into a bar or one of the many USO clubs, the girls never failed to leave their dates and sidle over to our group. Were we really that outstanding? I began to develop an ego problem when my mate explained that the young lasses knew we were on shore with 50 percent more pay than the other swabies. "Great," I enthused, "but how do they know?" "You stink, man," my buddy said. "I what?" "You stink. We all do. Don't you realize that six weeks, under water, in a diesel tube is going to leave its mark on you? We don't notice it, but the girls always do. Even in your clean, dress whites, those broads can smell you and the 50 percent extra pay you bring in." So I asked myself, "What's so bad about living in a tube with eighty-five other smelly guys?" We lost fifty-five of our subs in that war.

"Silent subs in Subic Bay, Philippines."

LEE STATH (MARILEES)

# Chapter IV

# Life Under Water

THIS WAS SHORTLY after the war had ended, and with those years spent under the sea, I was intrigued by a school teaching underwater salvage. Back in the late '40s, underwater dress had progressed little. Each diving shoe weighed 20 pounds. The leaded belt was 75 pounds. All this, added to the Mark V Mod 1, copper helmet, weighing 55 pounds, and I was staggering around deck with 170 pounds of dead weight. Yet, on the bottom, I was weightless and had to use caution not to over-inflate and blow to the surface. So I moved in slow motion, every task a monumental effort.

"Danger is my business or another day, another dive off the California coast."

After completing the schooling, I teamed up with a likeable fellow diver, Bert Elkins; and we bought a thirty-five-foot working boat, installed a massive compressor, and hoisted our diving gear aboard. We were ready for any salvage job or sunken treasure we might stumble upon.

Stumble would be the only way. Hollywood movies, showing divers in crystal-clear lagoons, ill-prepared us for the murky depths into which we worked.

We had long searched for an expensive Chris Craft boat that had gone down in the bay off San Pedro in California. Weeks we dredged, hoping to hook the elusive treasure. One sunny afternoon, a nearby fishing boat hailed us and said their nets were snagged, and if we could dislodge them, it would be worth $50. It took me half an hour to get dressed, but it was worth the dive. Just as we had hoped, their net was caught on the prize we sought; and there on a sandy bottom, in no more than forty-five feet, was our key to wealth. I freed their fouled fishing nets, and surfaced, and we dropped a marker buoy and looked forward to the task of tomorrow. I won't elaborate over the weeks and varying techniques employed in our efforts to raise this boat; towing it to the surface, cables slipped through the sand under the hull to lift it to the surface; four, flooded fifty-gallon drums attached to the hull and then blown dry with our compressors but still nothing moved. We were becoming quite an attraction to the local fishing community, which saw us dress each dawn, dive, and surface later after another failed attempt.

Here was another clear, sunny day. No wind. No waves. It was so pleasant that we were loathe to start the discouraging day's ritual. So, we sat idly on deck, watching the pelicans soar nearby. One lone, single-engine plane droned in the distance. We watched and marveled at his antics. He climbed high, turned in a giant arc, and then nosed down for a complete loop. Halfway through the maneuver, he was in trouble. The altitude was quickly, diminishing and the loop was incomplete. The plane shuddered, accelerated, and struggled to find height but smashed, instead, full force into that placid sea. There was no fire or explosion and from our distance only a small splash. We hauled anchor and made directly for the oil stain left as the only sign of the grisly episode. A quick check of the depth showed only thirty feet. Quicker and easier with face mask and swim fins, we were at the wreckage in moments. It lay, seemingly, gently in the soft, sandy bottom. The engine was crushed into the cockpit. I fished through the shattered windshield, and my groping hand found the long hair of a woman. I pulled her out, but when I pressed my face mask closer, I looked directly into her open eyes; but she had no body. I screamed underwater, or tried to, then rushed to the surface, gasping for air. Bert surfaced immediately, and I wailed, "Did you see?" "I did," he replied. "Let's go back down and bring them up." I dove under, reluctantly, and we resumed the unpleasant job of bringing up their mangled remains. Thank, God, there was no blood, only gray, lifeless matter. What must have started out as a gay, carefree morning for these two must have ended with a few terrifying moments before they discovered the answer to the universal question.

We continued working to raise our treasure, and our perseverance paid off when we proudly towed our prize into port amid a few cheers from our faithful onlookers. We weren't completely tied to the dock when two, dark-suited gentlemen strode down the pier and handed us some legal-looking papers and stated, simply, that as insurers of the salvaged Chris Craft, they were still the owners. There was a lot of protesting, but they were kind enough to say that, in the future, any salvage job we might undertake, we should first purchase the claim for one dollar and then the prize was legally ours.

LEE STATH (MARILEES)

# Chapter V

# A Star Is Born

I WAS BORN IN 1926; but I think life, for me, really began in 1952. I was in my senior year at Trinity University, a drama major with a minor in art and German. I had been struggling through the university almost since war's end. I would ease, casually through a semester, then kick-start my Harley Davidson and head out to California for another go at success and fame.

"Mr. Skin n' Bones at Muscle Beach back in the '40s."

I fell in with an elite group of body builders at the famed "Muscle Beach" in Santa Monica. They welcomed me into their "Muscle House by the Sea." It was a hedonistic atmosphere with Steve Reeves, Mr. America of 1947 and movie fame; George Eiferman, another Mr. America; and half a dozen other fanatics. It was just another day at the beach, weightlifting, hand balancing, and just browning our bodies in the West Coast sun.

It was on one of those days when MGM studios sent out a crew to pick up a dozen movie stand-ins. I joined the other eager, nonworking, beach bums for a ride to the studio. Once inside those hallowed halls, we were lined up, and, like prize cattle, checked out, accepted, or sent back to the beach. My turn went quickly. I was told to step aside and then, later, taken into the inner sanctum of the studios. I stood before a balding, bloated man who dominated the room though he remained seated behind his massive, polished desk. Surely, this must be Mr. MGM. He looked up, flicked cigar ashes on the plush carpet, and growled, "Yeah?" My escort pushed me forward and asked him, "What do you think?" I was casually scrutinized by Mr. MGM who leaned back in his overstuffed chair, eyeing me casually and finally replied, "Yeah, I see what you mean. Maybe so." He asked me, "You! Can you take falls from a horse?" "Yes, sir," I replied. "OK, we're looking for a Tyrone Power double. You might do." I was in. I had made the big time. Stardom was at hand. I returned to the beach to share this good fortune with my friends. I never heard another word from Mr. MGM.

Once again, I kicked my sweet Harley, bade adieu to California, picked up the old Route 66, and headed back to Texas and another semester at Trinity University.

"A man and his Harley somewhere out west on the old Route 66."

LEE STATH (MARILEES)

# Chapter VI

# Life Begins For Lee

**W**E WERE DOING a play rehearsal for Shakespeare's *The Tempest* when my co-actor told me of a trapeze act his father knew and had come down to San Antonio to winter and practice; we should go out and watch. And that was the beginning of my life. I watched in fascination as the flyers flew and the catcher caught. What a way to make a living. What a life that must be. After their practice, I asked if I might go up for the fun of it. My wish was granted, but it was no fun. I never realized forty feet could be so terrifying. I clung to the cables supporting the platform with such tenacity that the girl flyer thought it was a joke and climbed up to get a closer look at the clown. I was so numbed by fear that I never noticed this incredible beauty standing casually next to me. I shook my head, refused her challenge to "just swing off," and climbed, instead, awkwardly down the shaky ladder just in time to see her arch her supple, muscular body out into the air, pull into a double somersault, and drop tauntingly into the net. She rolled gracefully out, dropped to the ground, slipped past me, and said, "You're really funny." I had to be part of this.

I approached her husband cautiously; and here, at the age of twenty-five, never having seen a circus, I asked him if I could join up. "Actually, we've been looking for a man of your caliber." He winked to his catcher, Dave. "Really?" I choked. "Yeah, we need someone to shoot out of the cannon." Then, they all fell about laughing. A cruel circus joke, but I kept coming back each day. After their practice was done and permission granted, I undertook the daunting challenge of climbing those dizzying heights with the determination just to swing off on that trapeze and drop onto that narrow, ribbon of net, so far below. It was because of my perseverance, yet obvious acute case of acrophobia, that SHE, once again, climbed up beside me and began the tedious task of teaching me "the ropes." I loved her immediately.

The first of May rolled around. I graduated and got my bachelor's degree from Trinity and declined the prospect of teaching English and drama at a small school in a small town. Roy Valentine, Mary's husband, agreed that an extra working hand would be useful so I was allowed to join them for their first engagement in Chicago. I was eager and strong and did two men's share of dismantling the apparatus, pulling up the heavy iron stakes imbedded in the ground, lifting, and shoving the heavy steel tubing into the rigging truck until it was loaded; and I was ready to set out on my greatest adventure since the war.

I was positive I made a good impression on the act with my extra physical efforts. They showed no particular interest and insisted on calling me Moe. I guess I wasn't the first gung ho enlistee. Two or three weeks of donkey work and show business lost its glamour. I was certain that in such a prestigious and dangerous act, if I persevered, applied myself to any and all menial chores, and overcome my fear of heights, I would somehow fit into this fantastic world

LEE STATH (MARILEES)

called Circus. I took turns driving the big truck, while Mary drove the Cadillac, pulling the house trailer. We pressed on, altering our chores, and on one occasion found the two of us, together, in the back of the truck. She still didn't know my name, and the only time she spoke was to inform me that I was reading a magazine upside-down. *What magazine?* I could only see her. I dare make no overture; her two brothers were muscular chunks of gristle, and they held the new working boy in scant respect.

"Robert and Mary Atterbury of the Atterbury Circus ca. 1935."

The Atterbury boys were only two from a large, Catholic family of five boys and three girls. The father, Robert Lee Atterbury, was a circus owner and had allowed Mary and her older brother Robert to form their own act. He let them make their own contracts and travel where they liked. There was no question the kids had a big advantage with their father's name and reputation. Back in the 1920s when the circus moved, they had big trucks, wagons, and living trailers that inched their way across the northwest. It was on one such jump that Rose Atterbury (nee Heinz from Germany), the wife of Robert Lee, she was also a wire walker, dog trainer, and bareback rider (your average, circus haus frau), gave birth to Mary. Frau Rose had come over from Germany still quite young, but had never learned to trust or have time for hospitals, So, it was somewhere in Nebraska, they think near Omaha, that this gypsy vixen sprang forth, always her father's favorite and for good reason. Even as a small child, one could see the sensual beauty in the small, lithe body that was destined for circus fame. In America, Europe, or wherever she performed, throughout the world, she was unique. Her childhood was hardly normal. She began performing at the age of three. Her father would always single her out to accompany him on his trips to the city halls to obtain the necessary licenses and attend to the legal matters. Her innate suspicion and pessimism must have stemmed from watching the city fathers rubber-stamp the permits in exchange for a generous, under-the-table, donation. To this day, she has only contempt for those in power and public office.

I wasn't in power and had no craving for any kind of office; yet she treated me, not with contempt but more, and even more demeaning, complete indifference. That is, until we stopped for a break at a roadside diner. We all came in to an empty table; and I, without a thought, pulled out the chair for Mary to sit. She took the chair, and as she sat, she looked at me as if it were the first time she had seen me. "Thanks," she said. There was no other word between us, yet, that one word was sufficient to carry me all the way to Chicago and beyond. Once we arrived our lives took on, what I was yet to learn, the norm of the circus hierarchy. I was given a job as prop boy on the show. After we had put up the rigging for the Flying Romas (a contraction of Roy and Mary), I learned I must keep in my place. We, the working boys, did not mingle with the artists. I only saw Mary from a distance, but something had passed between us, many miles back in that roadside diner.

LEE STATH (MARILEES)

# Chapter VII

# The Big Time

HAVING ARRIVED IN Chicago and accepting my diminished role as "prop boy," I could see with the eyes of an outsider yet be close up with the artists I assisted. One memorable experience was handing the great Unus, the man who stands on one finger, his props during his act. Having been a hand balancer of sorts myself, I was much more astounded by his feats than the average layman in the audience. They truly believed the man achieved the impossible by doing a one hand stand supported only by his single, index finger. I, on the other hand, having practiced some years merely to accomplish a one-arm handstand, knew his trick to be just that, a "trick." Therein lies the wonder. Within five feet from this magician, I see him slip on his white gloves; place his finger onto the round, glowing lamp, and then lever into the "one-finger stand." Dressed in suit and tails, patent leather shoes pointed neatly together, he slowly removes his top hat with his free hand and holds the pose. I'm watching closely—the crowd is enthusiastic—and when he comes down, he slowly removes the glove and, for the doubting Thomas's, slaps it lightly, several times, across his other palm. "See, nothing inside." The audience was amazed. I was incredulous. I was so close. I could see everything. I saw nothing. What a great hand balancer. What a great performer. What a magician. What must it feel like to have a whole audience so impressed by your performance? How about a guest appearance on the great Ed Sullivan variety show?

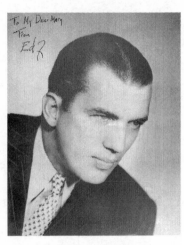

"Ed Sullivan acknowledges Mary."

That was my next introduction to the inner sanctum of the showbiz world. We, the Flying Romas, were laying off at the Hamid-Morton winter quarters in New Jersey. At that time of year, quite a few acts were idle. Not that I, personally, was idle. Roy kept me busy sanding rust and painting things that didn't move. That, plus driving the truck and other menial chores, seemed my only purpose. Some say I drove the truck quite well. But you know "idle hands" . . . So when the act next to us, Baudy's Greyhounds, an ebullient, robust Frenchman, and his wife Yvette, needed a helper with his pack of greyhounds and four mean chimpanzees during his engagement on the *Ed Sullivan Show*, I was eager and available. This was the Big Time. So off we went in his truck: Baudy, whistling with his elbow out the window; me, with my knees clenched tightly together; while Yvette sat, casually, between us with her hand resting, suggestively, on my crotch. But once in the studio, I was given my costume, a dingy gray oversized pair of coveralls and was told to clean out the cages. This I could do. Despite my lowly chores, I was witness to the marvel of early television and the superstars it enticed. I stood transfixed as the great (they were all great) Yehudi Menuhin sauntered casually by, Stradivarius in hand. Robert Merrill and Roberta Peters were on the bill, and Eartha Kitt even looked at me as I stumbled out of her way. But enough of this namedropping. It was showtime. Baudy and his Greyhounds performed at breakneck speed. The audience loved them. The chimps, however, were a surly bunch, tending to bite and defecate a lot. My job was to fend them off and clean up behind them. But to be on the same bill as these legendary stars was, surely, a hint of better things to come.

## Chapter VIII

# On The Road Again

*T*HE TREASURE OF *Sierra Madre*, I saw it once, I saw it twice, and I don't know how many more times; but how it caught my thirst for such drama. I was still an actor by wish and lived each scene with Humphry Bogart, John Huston (that great director), and Tim Holt.

"Tim Holt another star, another idol."

I could have played one of those roles and, in my reverie, did so. Years later, when my dream of stardom had turned to trapeze clown (I did start out as a funny flyer in my early trapeze career).

I was blown away when we were engaged at a small fair in Shade Gap, Pennsylvania; and the celebrity star, booked on the same bill, was Tim Holt. The year was 1952, some twenty-one years before his death at the early age of fifty-four. But what a rush of excitement to meet and talk with this same man I had seen and worshiped for his part in that memorable film. What a letdown it must have been for this once-prominent actor to be on the same bill as the other circus actors in Shade Gap, Pennsylvania. Perhaps fate had intervened and set me on the better path to stardom. I know things only improved for me from Shade Gap to Kerrville. It was there, in Shade Gap, that Roy Valentine, Mary's husband and boss of the act, and I finally faced each other with the fact that Mary and I were lovers. I was prepared for the worse, but all that happened was

"Always leave 'em laughing in Montreal 1952."

my prized guitar was smashed in the truck. "Must have happened on our last trip" was all that Roy would say. I was expecting a lot more. After all, I was sleeping with his wife. So at the close of Shade Gap, I was let go, told to take my meager belongings, and get on down the road. Mary drove me to the highway and said, "I'll see you in San Antone." Long road back home, but there was hope of a bright future. Some time passed. But for me, time stood still until Mary was back, and all was right in my adolescent life. Adolescent? I was twenty-six years old, a war veteran, ex-school teacher, and world traveler. But for me, this was the beginning of my life. I had found my purpose and the woman to whom the rest of my life would be dedicated. It was a long, sometimes turbulent, path that led, ultimately to serenity and happiness until her betrayal. But I get ahead of my story.

## Chapter IX

# Showdown At Fiesta San Antone

**B**ACK IN SAN Antonio, it was Fiesta time. This is a yearly event in spring, lasting ten days. It's the Texas equivalent of Mardi Gras, and Mary's brother had set up his joints (carnival booths) where I was working for him. It was a shooting gallery, and he was making a fortune. Hoards of people thronged the midway, and we couldn't take their money quickly enough. Suddenly, Roy was there. I had been expecting this inevitable confrontation ever since Shade Gap. Eb, Mary's brother, was trying to talk with him. Eb didn't like Roy, but not many people did. Still, I don't believe Eb liked me any better. After all, it was his sister. Roy called me out, and Eb pulled me aside to whisper, "Don't hit him first." Some carney wisdom that seemed foolish to me, but I really didn't relish the idea of a physical confrontation. Couldn't we discuss this like a civilized cuckold? He was drunk and grabbed my shirt, spewing his foul resentment in my face. I pulled away and pleaded, somewhat comically, "Don't hit me, Roy." That was the necessary catalyst; and he swung wildly, leaving himself open to a stiff right hand to his face. It hardly seemed fair. He went down, clutching me around the waist as he fell to the pavement. His nose was shattered, and he bathed my shirt front with his blood. Eb pushed me back and said, "Get the hell out of here." I took off like a deer through the gathering throng. I must have made a gory sight, dashing, blood-soaked through those festive onlookers. Finally, at some distance, I was overtaken and held captive by a number of concerned citizens. "What did he do?" "Hold him still." "Looks bad." "Get the police." The crowd was unanimous. I was bad. I felt subdued and was ready for my punishment when a rough-looking fellow pushed through the posse, took hold of both my shoulders, and barked, "Are you weisithit?" Carney talk. Thank, God, I had learned it during my association "with it." I answered in like tongue that I was indeed "one of them." He seized me from their grasp and shouted, "I'll take care of this. Come along, you." He tugged me off and away from what seemed a lynch mob. Once, safely out of sight, he wiped his hands on my shirt sleeves and said, "Now get out of here and get cleaned up."

Interesting note about this carnival argot. In their world, set so far apart from the "towners," the multitudes, the average working-class citizen, this close-knit group had found it necessary to invent a language by which they could communicate with one and other, while in the midst of the "towners" or outsiders and not be understood. I have no idea where it started, but it dates back to the early depression days and spread to England and Australia. It is simple, since simple people needed it. But it was used and gave identity to all who understood and spoke it. It came to my salvation, and I revel in its secrets. If I were to share this, I would be forced to change my identity.

# Chapter X

# The Big Show
# (as Viewed from Underneath)

FAST FORWARD SEVERAL months. The act had completed the '52 season; and Mary and I had reached a point where, it was obvious, I would not make it as a flyer. "You've got to learn about rigging and learn to be a catcher." With that, she contacted Art Concello, the general manager of the Ringling Circus; and I was accepted, once again, as a ring boy but on the "Big Show." This time, I came with a gray army blanket and a bit more knowledge of life on the road. Ringling Brothers Barnum and Bailey was known as the "Big Show." It was certainly my introduction into the ultimate of "showbiz." Once again, I was assigned a berth on the show train. This was much bigger and more crowded than the tiny bunk in the old truck I previously called home. Here, we were completely isolated from the performing artists. We were working men; and there was no artistry in these cramped, smelly, dimly lit compartments. But there was much gambling and heavy drinking with the pervasive smell of cheap tobacco and old sweat. Combine that atmosphere with the debauchery that took place on those long overnight jumps, from show ground to show ground. When small gangs of semi-criminals and would-be thugs would gang-rape the young effeminate boy who met their fancy and offered little resistance.

It was on the gilley ride, from the train to the lot, when one of the roughnecks singled out a newcomer sitting next to me and brandished a set of brass knuckles, muttering, "You'd better enjoy your teeth 'cause when we get off the bus, I'm taking them all out." He swaggered around and persisted in his threats as the boy cringed in his seat. It seemed the ride was interminable and the end too terrifying for the threatened boy. I had, for some time, taken to carrying a "black jack" fastened inside my waistband. One must realize that this was not your normal working class, and out of my normal character, I slapped the heavy leaded weapon against the palm of my hand and advised the bully he had best think again before doing anything silly. I didn't like the idea of a beef with him. I knew the frightened victim next to me would be of no assistance, but I felt an advantage with my weapon at arm's length over the aggressor's short muscular arms despite the "knuckles." We came to the lot, stopped, and began to unload. There were no partisans. Most of the Neanderthal working men were looking forward to the bloodletting. We faced off, the boy stayed behind me; and while I stiffened for the assault, our antagonist spewed vile threats of what we could expect on the next night's run. He turned away, his back to me, which I interpreted as submission or a temporary truce; and we broke off to take up our tasks of building up the tent.

It was through this kind of assertion, hard work, and knowledge of ropes, knots, splicing, and rigging that I achieved the enviable rank of head rigger for ring number three, big man among the working boys but a long way down the echelon of the circus caste system. Still fate, nay, sex was to intervene. Work done, tent guyed out, and ready for showtime, I stripped to my Levis, went to the cook house, and gave the cook a dime for a bucket of hot water and cleansed my body and soul. Chico sidled up and said there was a lady, in a new Cadillac, asking for me. I tried

"Put up day on the Ringling Bros. show in 1952."

to nod casually and said I'd be there soon. Now clean, fresh, and wearing a new, white T-shirt, I found Mary in the shiny black Caddy with Art Concello, the general manager of the show, leaning inside her window. He had, for several years, been beseeching Mary to join their show. The contract was for her to dictate, but Mary had a way of refusing without offending: perhaps some other time, always leaving an opening. I came to the car. Art turned and snarled, "What the hell do you want?" Oh, we both knew what I wanted; but fate, youth, and Irish good luck put me in the seat next to Mary. She smiled at Art then spun the wheels and took us off to the promised land. This was the beginning of a beautiful friendship.

LEE STATH (MARILEES)

# Chapter XI

# Circus City, Sarasota

I STUCK OUT the rest of that tortured tour and finished the season at the winter quarters in Sarasota, Florida. It had been a hectic, wild ride of six months; but I shared a bit of pride at this mammoth caravan moving cross-country with such speed and efficiency. So efficient that, in the late 1930s, the Germans sent over a group to travel with the show to learn how one could move such great bulk and so many personnel so rapidly from place to place. The Nazis put these lessons to good use in the years that followed, thus the Blitzkrieg.

Ironic how the Ringling Bros. Barnum and Bailey chose this small seaside village to set up their winter quarters. The railroad was convenient, and they built a spur directly into their vast acreage to serve the needs of a traveling railroad circus. In this vacant sandy saw palmetto waste, they transformed it into a sprawling beehive of welding shops, carriage builders, wardrobe designers and sewing rooms, massive cranes, and machinery capable of building their own railroad cars. Some of the coaches housed half a hundred workers. Others catered to a few select artists or "stars" in which the entire coach became a traveling suite. Buildings were erected to keep a full zoo full of exotic animals; huge arenas for practicing and fine-tuning the acts for the coming season. This was the biggest thing to ever come to this town. So it began to grow, an attraction that drew tourists and sightseers from all over the continent. The circus built not only its winter quarters; it also built a sprawling city out of Sarasota. It flourished for some time. Circus performers settled in, bought property, built homes. Sarasota was a circus city. Life was good, and everyone profited. Yet as the town expanded, more wealth arrived with speculators and retirees. The idea of "circus city" did not meet the image desired of the new residents. The Ringling museum was a godsend, a collection of fine art that brought connoisseurs and the genteel visitors in to become owners of wealthy homes and estates and a desire to rid their new domicile of, how would one phrase it, a circus atmosphere. And so the circus was figuratively run out of town.

They didn't have to run far—Down the road to Venice where they were welcomed enthusiastically with greedy open arms. Once again, they settled in and rebuilt complex accommodations for a massive circus training school and winter quarters. But many of the earlier performers, who had settled in Sarasota, ignored the pressure and eased into the good life along the Tamiami Trail.

LEE STATH (MARILEES)

# Chapter XII

# A Brand New Act

NOW, WITH THE Ringling Bros. experience behind me, I returned to San Antonio as a qualified rigger. Would Mary accept me as such? With her divorce finalized, she was free, and the word spread quickly. A telegram from Clayton Behee, a protégé of Alfredo Codona, and one of the finest flyers of this era, asking Mary to come to Lansing, Michigan, and join him and Eddy Cole with their new flying act on the Pollack Shrine Circus. The offer was good, and she promised to bring along her own rigger. That was me.

With just the Cadillac, we made good time, and after checking into the nearest hotel in Lansing, I was soon in the girders hanging the rigging for the Cole-Behee Flyers.

While I was doing my part aloft, Clayton and Eddie were in the ring having some dispute over something. In the ensuing scuffle, Clayton fell and dislocated his shoulder. Tragedy! Opening was tomorrow, and the principle leaper was finished. No need for concern. Lee—accomplished rigger— was also a flyer. I would take Clayton's place. Mary could see the absurdity of it and refused to participate. "I'll drop bars, but that's it. I don't want my name associated with this farce." Showtime and I was at my best. Unfortunately, my best was not very impressive. I did all the tricks in my repertoire, and the biggest one was a simple girlie trick. I was an embarrassment to the profession. It took the show a week to find an act to replace us, and then they sent us "on down the road."

With Clayton out, Mary and Eddie put their heads together and conceded, "This clown can't fly, maybe we can teach him to be a catcher." Eddie had been a very capable flyer on the Ringling show; but when his wife, Herta, had fallen and was pretty badly injured, he had the bad idea to sue "The Big Show" and make a fortune. He got some money, but he was persona non grata on most shows after that. Even though he had bulked up to 170 pounds, we all headed out to California to practice, teach me to catch, and introduce to the circus world the Flying Mary-Eddies.

Leaving Lansing, Mary reasoned, we couldn't afford to stay in motels. We needed a trailer. It was on a weekend, and she phoned one of her many contacts. At the dealers, she picked out a small eighteen-foot Yellowstone for $5,000. Sunday morning, they were at the bank. We had no money, no job, and no collateral. With Mary's word and not even a down payment, we hooked up and drove off for the Golden State with a new trailer behind. I was just tagging along; and once in California, Mary made arrangements with an old

"Roy Rogers and Mary with Trigger. Dale Evans was not on the scene."

LEE STATH (MARILEES)

friend, Roy Rogers, and we put up our rigging on his ranch to begin the tedious task of making me a catcher.

The following months were grueling. Eddie got a day job at the Ford factory, and I became a maintenance man at a local foundry. It was ambiguous, after a day of menial chores, to come outside the factory and find Mary waiting for me in the big Caddy. It's somewhat vague and unlike me at this time, but on my own, I went to see the Clyde Beatty Circus, which was showing nearby. I approached the great man himself, telling him of the marvelous Mary-Eddies. Mr. Beatty, knowing both Mary and Eddie, said, "Bring it on over to the next town, and we'll give it try." And so began the 1953 season for the Flying Mary-Eddies on the Clyde Beatty Circus.

"The Flying Mary-Eddies."

# Chapter XIII

# Clyde Beatty's Menagerie And Freak Show

IT IS NOW 1953, and I have had a full year of experience in a new profession. So much more to learn. Mary and I had had another falling out. I can't remember what about. It could have been the night show when I tried to grab a short, late (bad combination) double somersault. An experienced catcher would have left it alone, but I was still learning and trying to catch everything. Anyway, I got half of one hand and a few fingers of the other and pulled her down the hill with my accelerating swing. Well, when you pass through the bottom part of the arc, her 105 pounds becomes 205 pounds, and I lost her there. Bad place to come off. Instead of falling straight down, she was ripped off like a slingshot and skidded ass first along the net. I know it looks soft, and it is when you plop straight down, but when you are up to speed, it turns into a cheese grater. I heard the roar of the crowd; and when I looked down, I saw her rumpled sequined costume in the net and a few feet further, my lovely wife was getting up, stripped nude except for her jockstrap. Girl flyers wear them too, you know. That could have been the reason. But when you're working that close together, day in and day out, it doesn't take a lot to create a little tension. I know, she was a twenty-year veteran and I was a "First of May" (a term I'll explain in more detail later); but the haranguing, criticism, and tongue-lashing was too much. I took my Levis and razor and left the trailer that night. I went to the horse tent and bedded down in the straw.

Next morning, the show was moving, so I asked Mr. Beatty if there was a bunk on the train. He said he would fix me up but only after I assured him I would be catching the act in the next town. So I moved my meager belongings into my new home on the circus train. Fortunately, my belongings were meager as my new dwelling was an upper bunk with mattress, room at the foot of the bed to pile one's clothes on and a curtain for privacy. Who could ask for more? In the Second War, I'd spent two years in much less space. But on board, my shipmates were all volunteers, carefully culled and the elite of the fleet. Here, on the circus train, I eventually found my traveling companions to each possess individual traits and personalities that set them far apart from ones daily acquaintances. KARL, "The Man With Two Faces." The coach, in which I was assigned, was not entirely for performing artists. Clyde Beatty also had a freak show on the midway.

Karl was a member of that unique group and had the bunk

"Typical side show front on a circus mid-way."

across the aisle. We had not yet met. That introduction took place the next morning as we neared the town of Lamont just south of Bakersfield in California. I managed to squirm into my Levis, pulled my curtain aside, and there was Karl, standing in the aisle, already dressed for the day.

I said, "Morning." And to this day, I pride myself on the composure I displayed when he turned around and made some indistinguishable sound of greeting. Karl, "The Man With Two Faces," had not yet put on his second face. During his act, he was displayed to the audience with a plastic mask that covered all of his lower face, leaving only his eyes, forehead, and a surprising amount of thick brown hair that he kept tied in a knot at the back of his head. After a good bit of ballyhoo from the barker, explaining the misfortune Karl had suffered in a chemical explosion while working for the Secret Service, Karl would rip off his plastic shield and expose himself. It was not a pretty sight. It was gruesome. Just beneath his normal eyes, where the cheekbones and nose should have been,—there was nothing, only a deep cavity that extended down to his throat: no mouth, no chin, no teeth, no face. This was the roommate that greeted me that first morning. But there was more to come, a lot more. Karl moved down the passageway to the donniker at the far end. (Donniker is the circus term for the restroom. I've been unable to find the origin of the word, but I use it still.) His absence was quickly filled by an abundance of flesh. It was Paulo or "Maurice The Mountain Man" as he was billed. By today's standards, he was a lightweight; but back in the early '50s, 400 pounds of fat was enough to make him an oddity. He wore a flowery gown or sort of Mu Mu. He stretched, yawned, and farted loudly.

That struck him as extremely humorous, and he giggled in a high falsetto voice that hinted to his sexual orientation. "Asshole!" hissed a genuine feminine voice, a few bunks down; and out slid Blanche with not sufficient clothing, or so I felt, for such a public presentation. So here at my feet, as I still sat, half out of my upper bunk, I'd met or seen "The Fat Boy From Phoenix"; Karl, "The Man With Two Faces"; and Blanche, the nymphet with two breasts. There were, of course, many more characters and oddities in our coach: the Bearded Lady, the Human Skeleton, the sword swallower, the fire-eater, and half a dozen showgirls sprinkled throughout the compartment. Nevertheless, those three were the first I'd seen, and all left a permanent impression on me. In some ways, I wished I was back in the horse tent. In every way, I wished desperately that I could be back in the trailer with Mary.

The train pulled into town, and we all disembarked. I caught a ride to the lot on a tractor, while most waited around for the gilley (a circus bus of transport). I was eager to get to the tent and start building up our rigging. Most of the stakes for the guy lines were driven into the ground for us, but the putting up of our flying trapeze, we trusted to no one. Eddie Kohl, our other flyer, was already there, having come by road with his trailer. Now here we were, all together, Eddie, Herta, Mary, and me, "The Flying Mary-Eddies." Herta didn't do much. She was never quite the same after her fall. Eddie was a handsome curly-haired blond guy, but the idle layoff time had added unwanted flesh to his frame. Now he was a hefty flyer, while I weighed in at only 150 pounds of gristle, which made for a real challenge on my body and ability or lack thereof.

Despite my eagerness and determination, whenever I missed a trick, Mary would bolster my ego by shouting, "You can't even catch a cold." Even so, Eddie could still turn over while Mary was our "feature leaper." Success had to lie ahead.

Showtime and there was a lot more to do than just fly around. Most acts had to do "two or more" to compete on a circus for a contract. That meant you did, for example, your feature number and then threw in a roustabout clown number or some such secondary act. Everyone went into Spec (the spectacular parade that started the show). We, being the elitists that a flying act is proclaimed, did just the one act. But to make ourselves secure and earn a bit more money, we took advantage of "Cherry Pie." After the show was over, the fairyland turned into a grim labor camp. Sequined ballet dancers became burdened bearers of heavy canvas as wild beast tamers meekly loaded seats on awaiting wagons; while we, the eagles of the air, cleaned up the animal dung.

The act went well tonight. At least "Old Butter Fingers" didn't miss anything but that didn't mean Mary was going to laud me with praise. After we dressed, I said, "I guess I'll be heading back to the train." That was met with stony silence. Oh, how she could twist the blade. She gathered up my sweaty tights and flounced out of the dressing room. *I guess I'll be heading back to the train*, I mused and off I trudged.

The gilley dropped a bunch of us at the slumbering train and we dispersed to our various wagons. I was in no mood to settle in with Karl and was equally apprehensive of Blanche and the Fat Boy who both seemed to have designs on my body. It was going to be an overnight jump and I knew sleep

LEE STATH (MARILEES)

would be a challenge so I ambled down the few coaches to the pie car. Things were always lively here after tear down and the car was full of thirsty artists and hungry gamblers. There was always a card game in progress and the general atmosphere was jovial with a great deal of camaraderie. I was not yet a part of this closed society so I sat quietly in a corner with my Pepsi and wished I could join.

Always the center of the gathering was the two Hanneford brothers. They were the nucleus of The Hanneford Riding Troupe along with their younger sister Kay. But the mother and father were still in the ring after many, many years. There was always a bit of snickering backstage when, after the applause died down, the boys would bring the elderly mother back out and present her, with a near plea, for more applause. They were truly the masters of milking.

The train pulled out and the night wore on. Kay was in the pie car but always under the watchful eyes of her two brothers. She was of age and rightfully on her own but not in a close-knit family act. They would take no risks at losing an integral part of their number. It had long been a fact that she was hot for one of the candy butchers and he would sneak in to see her at every opportunity. Yet, intimacy was limited in the horse tent and she dare not be caught on the midway with him. On this long, overnight jump, he made the mistake of going into the Hanneford's wagon to see her. George and Tommy, the two brothers, caught him and beat him senseless and with the train at full speed, he was thrown out into the night. And this was the circus society I wanted to be a part of?

One other little perk was "sitting web." Every show had a production number featuring one of the glamour single trapeze artists. But before her entrance, the hippodrome track was filled with maybe twenty "web broads." These were the young girls who climbed the soft web ropes hung from the big top and performed, in unison, pretty gymnastic tricks.

To assist this was a "web sitter" who held the rope taut, slacked it when necessary, and spun it for the big finish.

I was splicing some cable in the ring when Blanche, the two-breasted broad, jumped onto the ring curb and said, "Hi." Simple overture, but I felt intimidated. "Whatcha doing?" "Just fixing some rigging," I answered. She slid over the ring curb and sat down next to me. "How would you like to sit for me?" she whispered. Now I knew what she meant. It was routine to pick out your web sitter; but the intonations, the covert nuances, left me in little doubt of what she wanted me to do. I had to get off that train and

"One of the lovelier web broads."

back in the trailer with Mary and quick. I did sit web for Blanche; she tipped me well each week, as was the custom; and I made amends with Mary. Life was good again, at least for the moment.

How quickly the moments pass. I know I set Mary on a pedestal and idolized her very existence, but she did have one flaw: she was too beautiful, too beautiful for me. I felt so undeserving of her love. I felt so insecure in her domain. I felt suspicious of every male. I was insanely jealous. As we partied after an early show one night and I sat sullen and silent in their midst, one tipsy friend said, "Hey, why don't you two get married and make an honest man out of Lee?" It was a blur, but we were across the border and into Tijuana where we found a bar with a justice of peace who said marriage was his game. Our names were taken. I gave him fifty pesos. He stamped the certificate and said, "Next?" So we were man and wife.

Back on the lot, alone in our trailer, I continued harassing her, accusing her of infidelity and treating her like the jerk that I was. She wasn't used to this kind of hostility, and before we knew it, we were acting like a married couple. Ugly things were shouted, and in my rage, I tore off her nightgown. She bolted out of the door, completely nude and cursing me, my mother, and all in general and ran shrieking down the deserted midway. Unfortunately, it didn't go completely unnoticed. The next day, Mr. Beatty called Eddie and I up to his office and paid us off. As much as he liked the act, he couldn't stand for my actions. Thus, ended the short life of the Flying Mari-Eddies.

# Chapter XIV

# We Are Not Carnival People (Yet if the Pay Is Right . . .)

WE TOOK OUR share of the rigging. Does that sound strange, our share of the rigging? Breaking up an act is all too similar to an ugly divorce. I knew one flying act that cut, literally, with a hack saw, their rigging in small pieces to divide it up between themselves. Such is the overpowering emotions that combine to make up this tenuous relationship between flyers and catchers. At least we had the net and a few whole sections of tubing. With these few possessions, we headed back to Texas to start a new life and another act.

Back in San Antonio, I called upon my old football coach, Jimmy Dugger, asking if he knew of any likely young athlete. Enter Roger Mireles, a sullen Mexican kid of seventeen with some potential and an attitude. With no father, he clung desperately to Mary and I as his family. We made poor substitutes, but still, we were able to draw forth an acceptable flyer from his raw athleticism. Through our rigid regime his scrawny body soon morphed into a near David type physic. He was a definite visual asset, but he had one major flaw. He was undependable, more of that later, much more.

When we finally got Roger airborne, Mary got in touch with a local carnival and sold the new "Flying Marilees" to be the "free act." We would set up our rigging at the far end of the midway and lure the throngs down to see what was going on. We opened one gray damp day in Cibolo, Texas. It couldn't have been more than twenty miles out of San Antonio, but we were on the road with our own act at last. I remember the date well as it was the first of May. That is a significant day in show business as it is the most ideal time of year to open and start the new season. That may be the birth of the term "First of May," a derogatory name given any newcomer to the circus world.

We opened on a fine drizzly day; while the owner, Mr. Jack Rubeck, joined a handful of carnival workers to watch our first performance. That was probably the biggest audience we ever had for that engagement. He made no comment, but he didn't fire us either. We were working pro rata, no play no pay. We knew that much about the vagaries of showbiz and soon took to checking the weather forecasts daily. We hung around the front of the midway, counting each customer that straggled by. Things were bound to get better. Please let us work. Even without an audience, we would go up and practice for an hour. Roger and I both were still learning. Perhaps out of sympathy, Mr. Rubeck let Mary have the "penny pitch" concession. She had lost none of her ability at slight of hand or as a short change artist. At least we could eat.

Conscious of my "lump on a log" status, I sought some means to earn my keep. See Isaac I was told. Isaac Aldrich was your typical carnie. A balding fat man with a huge cigar and a rasping voice, he agreed he could use someone on his weight guessing joint and introduced me to the complexities of the game. I was certainly qualified as it took no skill. My job was to lure the customers in with the challenge of guessing their weight with-in three pounds or they would win their choice of any of the grand prizes alluringly displayed. At only twenty five cents a chance the offer was too great to refuse. I proved to be the world's worse weight guesser and customer after customer walked away with their choice of any of the colorful gypsum trinkets that Isaac had purchased at ten dollars a gross or roughly seven cents each. I was a good looser, the towners were happy to have put one over on Mr. Smart Ass and Isaac was getting richer and growing fatter.

Then the show moved a few miles to the little town of Schertz. We loaded our soggy gear and followed. Maybe business would pick up. But my ear was good enough to know that "Schertz" was German for "joke" or "prank." Sadly enough that's what the date turned out to be. We were honing our profession but getting poorer in the process.

Then Mary did it again. One of her agent friends put her in contact with the Bodart Blue Ribbon Shows in Wisconsin. They could use a free act. Mary signed the contract and Mr. Rubeck was willing to let us go. A final touching gesture on the shows part was when all the carnies took up a collection to give us gas money for the long trip to Wisconsin. This was the beginning of a beautiful act.

Circus life now moved serenely along. Easily established with Mary's beauty and physical achievements plus all her theatrical contacts, we had little trouble obtaining choice contracts. "How about Ringling Bros?" Roger and I both chorused. "Not while I'm working," Mary bluntly stated. "You

LEE STATH (MARILEES)

First of Mays can go there when there's no other place to go, but I won't be associated with that old retirement home." So she got us lucrative bookings on the Shrine circuses. We did hopscotch from Mexico City up to Chicoutimi, Canada but we were working steady and getting paid.

A two-week layoff and nowhere to practice. Mary came back to the trailer and said "Get your wardrobe ready. We open tomorrow night in Jericho, Long Island." "What show

"Always top billing. Eat your heart out, Basil Rathbone."

is that?" I asked. "It's a drive-in movie theater. We put our rigging up in front of the screen, do one performance, and then tear it down." *Only one show and a full week's pay. Now that's the way to work*, I thought. We were packed and ready to go. Arrived early at the Westbury Drive-In and had the rigging set, waiting for sundown and the arrival of the fleet of autos, eager to see the show and our act. The cars arrived by the hundreds, filling the drive-in, but so did a torrential downpour. It was a deluge. The owner asked us to hang on. The autos honked impatiently. After a half hour with no let-up the man said it was a no-show. He couldn't expect us to work under those conditions, but he assured us he would honor the contract and pay. We were dressed for the act, so Mary said, "Let us go up at least. We'll see what we can do." We slogged out to the rigging. I slithered up the rope, and we tried a simple trick first. Mary and Roger powdered their hands and wrists with copious amounts of resin. We tried another trick and then another, and before the owner's astonishment and ours, we did the entire act. Dropped into the soggy net and we're met not by thunderous applause but by a cacophony of auto horns. Basil Rathbone, starring in *The Black Sleep*, had a tough act to follow.

With winter upon us, we hustled south to Mexico. It was here in Mexico City for the Christmas season of 1955 that Roger gave the first hint of what would prove to be a glimpse of true character, or perhaps lack of proper circus indoctrination. We had worked a week, perhaps, in this wonderful, permanent tenting engagement and doing shows daily to packed houses. Sunday warranted three shows, and the first was at ten thirty in the morning. Act time and Roger was a no-show. What could be worse? As luck would rear its lovely head, the Flying Ibarras, who lived in Mexico City, were visiting; and Vincente quickly pulled on a pair of our tights and jumped in to save the act. Sad to say, that was not the last time I was beholding to the Ibarras. However, to add to the irony, during the act, I looked in the top row of seats and there sat Roger, enjoying the performance. He never made any excuse or explanation, but that was Roger.

During our engagement with the Atayde Circus, we were in the middle of our act, before a rapt audience, when in walked Cantiflas, Mexico's answer to Charlie Chaplin. The house was in an uproar, and all eyes were for him only. I was hanging upside down, waiting for a trick, when Mary swung off and dropped flat into the net, rolled out, and walked to the exit. I had no choice but to follow suit, and the act was over, but I don't think anyone noticed. So much for our triumphal showing in Mexico, but there were bigger days to come.

A more amusing incident happened in the French-speaking part of Canada. We had been cautioned that they spoke French and only French. Forewarned, I was prepared not to offend, and though my high school French was meager and mostly forgotten, I eased into a small cafe and ordered, "Un café, sil vous plait." Sure enough, I got a cup of hot coffee and a SEA FOOD PLATE. Actually, it was quite tasty, even though it was still morning and I wasn't very hungry.

## Chapter XV

# You Follow The Chimp Act

THE HIGH POINT of our Canadian engagement came during an outdoor show in Windsor. Word had filtered down among the artists that Mrs. Kathleen Williams, the impresario from England, was coming over to see our act, first hand, with the possibility of a six-month engagement. Europe had long been my dream and goal. I had heard from all the foreign acts, with whom we had worked, of the vast difference between European circuses versus the American. I was avid to see for myself. Even Mary expressed a curiosity. Her only previous overseas experience had been as a young girl of fifteen, working with an all-girl high-wire act in South America. Strange that I can remember the name of the woman who made and chaperoned the act, Mamie Butters. And that was almost twenty years before my time. So with Mrs. Williams coming all the way over to see the Flying Marilees, I was in a state of terror. This had nothing to do with my acrophobia and the fear of falling, but much worse was the fear of failing. So much depended on impressing this renowned circus director. To me, our whole future depended on presenting an impressive act. With just the one performance, there would be no second chance. Showtime came, and we did a flawless number. Afterward, I was so tense and numb, my mouth so dry, I couldn't speak. It was left to Mary's intervention and experience that netted us the summer season of 1957 with the Tower Circus in Blackpool, England.

First, let's finish off our contract in America. We had a week's engagement at the Kennywood Park in Pittsburg. There was a stage set out on the edge of the lake, and our rigging just fit with the catch end looking down on the shimmering water below. It was really an idyllic setting: a small rustic wooden bridge led out to the stage, and we would stand there watching the first act go through their routine. I was fascinated by the spiderwebs connecting the wooden beams and the large spiders waiting patiently for one of the many buzzing insects to trip into their sticky traps. I almost missed our introduction, mesmerized by this life and death struggle, a tough act to follow.

Meanwhile, across town, the Ringling Brothers Barnum and Bailey were having their own struggle. But this was with the labor unions, and the show was no longer able to operate with the demands made by the union leaders. Sadly, on July 16, 1956, the Big Show folded its tents for the last time and headed off into history.

Our own problems were not so dire. We closed our show at midnight in Pittsburg and had a four-hundred-mile overnight jump to the Palisades Park in New Jersey to open the next day. Me, Mary, and Roger worked until 2:00 am, tearing down and loading the rigging. We had compromised a local pharmacist to slip us the needed narcotics to keep us awake for the long haul. After the act, the tear down, and loading, we were exhausted and ready for bed even before we started out. But the nightmare ended, or began, only when we arrived the next morning. It was just ten thirty, yet the prop boss was swearing and running in small circles shouting, "We open with a matinee in five hours. Get it up! Get it up!" I didn't have the energy to punch him so, instead, I started the ordeal of setting up those two tons of scrap iron into a symmetrical aesthetic array of aerial artistry.

There were, as usual, complicating statistics: the stage was so many meters long; we needed so many meters; the orchestra needed so many meters and at the end of the stage was a sheer drop of fifteen meters that should be avoided at all cost. Suddenly, it was 2:30 pm, and the hoards began storming in as I pulled the last guy wire taut, but we were ready. Mary had the wardrobe washed and dried, laid out, and ready. Breakfast, lunch, or whatever was never considered. Then the emcee asked if I had rehearsed my music. Of course, I hadn't. So he introduced me to Stan "The Man" Kenton. This was all too much. He had long been my idol. I stood before him, slumped shoulders, dirty coveralls, yet still in awe. I heard him asking "How many pieces you got, man?" As the Parks entertainment orchestra for that week, he was obliged to accompany our act. I handed him our music but was too tired to genuflect. So we flew, he played, and we tore the house down: me, the Marilees, and Stan Kenton. What a great engagement we had for ten full days.

It was still July, and we were in New Jersey, and it was hot. As fate would have it, the act booked the previous week was Ira Watkins and his chimpanzees. We knew Ira and we knew his chimps. Ira talked a lot and his chimps shit a lot. When we parked our truck and trailer at the designated spot, we knew Ira and his chimps had left their mark. As the

LEE STATH (MARILEES)

day grew on, the sun rose higher, and the park came to life. Children and adults frolicked in the summer sun. Back in our non-air-conditioned trailer (remember, this was back in the 50s), we tried vainly to find some needed sleep. But Ira and his chimps had left a lasting and growing impression on us. From the park, we could see the blue water of the Atlantic seemingly so near, yet there was no escape from the stench of chimp defecation steaming in the noon day sun. God bless you, Ira. We've seen your act often, and it was good. But no offense intended; your act stinks! Then again, how would you like to be on the same bill following "Le Petomane?"

# Chapter XVI

# Mary Buttercup

I HAVE A PHOTO of Mary. Actually, it's more like a work of art. Maybe I'm blinded by Mary. Maybe her beauty is imprinted on my eyes like the afterglow of a lightning flash. I think it will always be there. I hope it will always be there. But this particular photo was taken during

a performance. She was unaware of any cameras, and it certainly wasn't a photo op. Still, there she is, caught in mid-air, just as she is returning from the catcher to the trapeze. One hand is on the bar; the other still free. Her head is turned slightly toward the camera, and her flowing blonde hair creates a halo around her smile of triumph over gravity. Of the hundreds of shots I keep of her, this one remains my most treasured.

"Mary in the air."

# Chapter XVII

# Uncharted Waters

THE TIME HAD come to move out upon that blue Atlantic Ocean; move farther afield; and test our talents in deeper waters. That test took place in Blackpool, England. Blackpool was a blue-collar working man's holiday resort. It was made up, primarily, of bed and breakfasts, boarding houses, and hotels. Every week, the entire city was host to a new deluge of tourists. This went on, uninterrupted, for twenty-four weeks. What a boon for Blackpool. Besides the Tower Circus, there were twenty theaters with live shows. All the big, English and American entertainers vied for top billing. Singers, dancers, movie stars, comedians, groups (Rolling Stones were young then) all jockeyed for recognition during the Blackpool season. The Tower Circus was unique in that it was nestled in the basement of what was a replica of the Eiffel Tower but at 518 feet, only half the height. It

"Blackpool Tower."

was so prominent, sitting on the shore of the Irish Sea, that during the war, the Germans left it untouched as it served them so well as a landmark on their countless bombing sorties.

Here, in this fairyland basement, lay the most beautiful circus imaginable. Seating was covered in plush, red velvet. The ceiling was elaborately decorated in gold leaf. The single circus ring could be lowered, hydraulically, to allow a water tableau of show girls, gondolas and dancing waters. Our rigging fit so snuggly that we were almost within touching distance with the audience in the balconies. There were no candy butchers, no flashing toy lights or popcorn. On opening night, the front loges were occupied by patrons in evening gowns, tuxedos, and iced champagne buckets. Every show was packed, and when the midsummer season began, they added a third performance daily. This one began at ten thirty in the morning, but we were mollified by an increase of one third our daily salary, all this with no traveling, no rigging to wrestle, and the comforts of a plush apartment. Yet I believe the biggest perk was that the Tower Circus was a showplace that invited all the big circus owners and agents to witness this vast array of theatrical talents. It was during this one European engagement that I booked our act for four years in advance. That meant

"Interior of Tower Circus showing Flying Marilees performing."

1958 with Boswell Circus in South Africa, 1959 with Circus Knie in Switzerland, 1960 with Circus Schumann in Denmark, and 1961 for Circus Krone in Germany. Our future was laid out before us. My cup runneth over.

Closing in Blackpool, we had time to kill. That's a misnomer; we had time to enjoy, time to relax, time to enjoy the wonders of London, the Tate Gallery, Paris and the Louvre, Pigalle, and more. We arrived in Paris by rail, after an exhilarating, choppy channel crossing and at the Gare du Nord we had our first encounter with the, all-too-frequent union disorders. There was a taxi strike. Our hotel was booked, but we stood forlornly in the streets, baggage in hand with no means of getting there. That's when Mary, stepped out in traffic and hailed a passing motorist. He stopped (were these the French we had heard so many ugly stories about?), opened his boot (trunk), stowed our baggage, and drove us directly to our hotel. After helping me unload, he kissed Mary's hand (they did that a lot over there) edged back into traffic; and we were safely at our first French hotel, the Blanch Fontaine.

# Chapter XVIII

# Into Darkest Africa

HOLIDAY TIME PASSED quickly and we were suddenly on board the Union Castle Mail Boat, out of Southampton, bound for South Africa. Arriving in Cape Town, I could hardly wait to get settled so I could write my landlocked childhood buddy and quote, glowingly from Arthur Miller's play, *Death of a Salesman* Uncle Ben's great line, "The jungle is dark but full of diamonds, Willy." I was so smitten by this exotic new country, truly a land of enchantment and adventure. Besides the previously mentioned misadventure in the Kalahari Desert, there were other equally interesting happenings and new friends to be made.

"Boswell Circus set up on the shore below Table Mountain in Cape Town, South Africa in 1958."

Tommy Turnbull, he was a big robust Afrikaner. Another ex-acrobat turned clown, but in his case, he was a very funny clown. He had taken on the tramp make up and wardrobe so popular after Emit Kelly and Otto Grieblin had immortalized it back on the Ringling Show in the 40s and 50s. But here in South Africa, it was new. I learned a lot about juggling from Tommy. Between acts, we would gather outside our dressing rooms and compete with variations of three balls, four balls, and my feeble attempt at five balls. The native working boys were a great audience, but I wonder still if their unbridled hilarity over our antics was genuine or if they were masking their contempt at the white mans follies. You could never tell about the working boys. They were gathered from many different tribes in Africa, half a hundred strong and living together in an uneasy truce that often erupted into short brutal confrontations of alarming violence: clubs, knives, stout sticks, and occasionally bare fists. The strength was there and surely the hatred.

"Our working boy, *Gorilla*, and our 250 pound net."

This was in the 50s and apartheid was strongly enforced. In town, at the railway stations or wherever the two races were intermingling, the obvious was stated boldly with drinking fountains and rest rooms emblazoned with "European" or "Native." I remember my embarrassment and the policeman's amusement when Mary danced over to him and said, "I've got to pee, and I'm an American. Where the hell do I go?"

Back on the show, the boys were always there to do ones bidding: water to be carried, garbage to be disposed of; no chore was beneath them since the white boss was obligated and sometimes generous in their rewards. Money was good, but the main currency was cigarettes. Whenever a chore had been done, the boy would extend both cupped hands in front of him. It looked as if he was expecting much more than the five cigarettes I had been instructed to give him. But the response was always the same, "Thank you, Boss." It was a bit later I learned that this form of acceptance, this near genuflecting, was a result of the Afrikaner's insistence of seeing both hands of the black warrior, no hidden weapons behind their back.

We heard often the story of the faithful servant, grown up in the household, treated honestly, fairly, and loved. The rumor was always there of the day the blacks would rise up and slay their white masters. The mistress of the home would ask the faithful servant, "If that day were to come, Samuel, could you kill me and our family?" "Oh no, Missy," came the naive reply. "Botha, next door, would kill you, and I must kill his family." How innocent yet frightening yet not completely without understanding. I remember a large khaki-dressed Boer standing near us as we marveled at the immensity and wonder of Victoria Falls, "the River that Smokes." He stood at the railing and hailed a young passing native. "Hey, Kafir!" which is about the equivalent to our "nigger." "Come here." He did so, knelt down, and tied the fat man's shoe, as told, and then hurried off. No cigarettes but perhaps thankful no harm had befallen him.

That was nothing like our first encounter, farther north in what was then the Belgium Congo, with a tribe of Watussi warriors. Talk about intimidation. With me stretching to make five foot ten inches and Mary, blending into the sand, at five foot one inch, we were, well, intimidated. The proverbial ten foot tall did not seem exaggerated. Thank, God, they were here only to amuse us and not, as I feared, eat us or worse yet rape us both. I gingerly approached the one slender aloof-looking savage who was standing on only one foot while leaning on an eight-foot spear. I realized then that he was not ten feet tall but only an average six foot nine inches or so. His skin coloring was not bluish black but more of a bronze. Did it glow or was it the sun. Perhaps it was Max Factor? I sensed he disapproved of me, so for the moment, I felt safe from gang rape. I indicated we would like a photo taken with him. Seemingly, not an unusual request as he turned to his others and brought forth a regally attired Watussi warrior. He was adorned in colorful beads, carried the mandatory spear and hardly enough loin cloth to conceal his disdain for me and his lust for Mary. We got the photo. I proffered a generous ten cigarettes, which he rolled over in his hand before dropping them contemptuously on the ground. This was obviously the wrong currency. The big guy came back out, reached into his crotch, and pulled out a note of South African Rand and indicated for me to add to it. I hastily put in my ante of 10 Rand, and we were home free. We eagerly returned to the circus where I was greatly relieved to see normal-size blacks running around and calling me "Boss."

"Now, altogether gang, *Who's your boss?*"

# Chapter XIX

# Hanging by a Thread

**B**ACK IN 1952, when I graduated from Trinity U I received not only my BA diploma but also a beautiful gold ring with a sizable ruby in the center. I did cherish this token of achievement and wore it, even while working. This was resented by the flyers I caught, and they complained about it digging into their wrists when I clamped onto them with the "Lee death grip." But I was loathe to remove it. Through the years of strenuous work, I doubt if it could have been wrenched over my enlarged knuckles. I'll always wear my graduation ring. Then one night, after tearing down the rigging, I closed the metal door on our dressing room wagon. With the steps already having been loaded, I jumped down, but my ring caught in the metal door ledge. I hung there, by my ring finger, until some of the boys lifted me free. Lovely ruby ring had cut deep into the flesh of my finger, and I was going to need help in getting it off. Late night in Africa and we found a medic who tried, first, to cut off the ring. It was too thick and unyielding. Bite the bullet, and after several injections to deaden my lacerated finger, he managed somehow to work the ring over the flap of flesh and enlarged knuckle. He declined payment and on returning my ring advised me to get plenty of rest, keep my hand iced and elevated, and it should be OK. Back on the train, elevation was no problem. But ice? Come on. We're on a circus in Africa. The following day, there was no matinee so that gave me plenty of rest. But there was no way I could miss the night show because of a sore finger. I knew I couldn't climb up the rope to my trapeze, hand over hand. So I had the boys hoist me up by a pulley. Once there, I was home, and the act went well. The ring? Once healed, I worked it back on that scarred digit and wore it proudly.

"On my way to work."

# Chapter XX

# Another Opening, Another Show

ARLIER, WE HAD been in Durban and pampered ourselves with a stay at the Grand Hotel while the circus was presented for two full weeks and only a short walk away. We were living the life of your average family: clean sheets, flush toilet, hot and cold running water, and only a short walk to the circus. That's when this scroungy kid knocked on our door and said, "I'm Keith Anderson and I want to be a flyer." A disreputable-looking lad but with obvious intelligence, he not only spoke his English with a cultured English accent but was also fluent in Afrikaans. Thank goodness we were not at that moment in need of a flyer. I was polite and generously offered him time and instructions. He was eager and intent but without any innate ability. Closing in Durban and moving on, we were surprised to find him sitting on the next lot waiting for us. This continued for several weeks, and his will and determination to become a flyer was impressive. He had friends at the YMCA in Cape Town, and he was certain he could put up some rigging to practice with all the kids if he only had a net. His story was stale. I had had too many fledglings with the same gung-ho spirit and watched them wither by the wayside. I felt I had done enough when Mary stepped in and said, "We have an old net in England. You're welcome to it if you can get it to Cape Town." And that was the last we saw of him or so I believed.

Another long and profitable season was drawing to a close. The memory of past seasons in the United States when we would boast of twenty-six weeks work, making countless phone calls, telegrams, agent's fees, and the thousands of miles driven was slowly becoming an unpleasant memory. Here, we had just completed fifty-two weeks of uninterrupted work and blithely riding the rails carefree. But now it was time to move on; contract was fulfilled. Mr. Boswell, fearing we were anxious to leave, exercised the contract clause wherein he had the right to prolong our number for an additional four weeks. He wanted our act desperately for the Christmas opening in Johannesburg. We had nothing until early spring in Switzerland so it was perfect for us. He was unaware of this, and in an effort to sweeten the pot, he offered to pay our way back to England via the eastern route and in first class. Mary said we'd think it over. Let him stew. After three days, I eagerly accepted, and we rented a penthouse, overlooking the circus lot in Johannesburg.

Unfortunately, shortly before Christmas opening, I fell ill with some sort of malady that forced me to bed. Unable to rise, Mary and Roger somehow got the rigging up and ready for the grand opening; but I was too weak to stand. Mr. Boswell, always the enterprising entrepreneur, called in a doctor friend; and I was given two injections of something. Whatever it was, I wouldn't want to give a urine sample afterward. Showtime. I went up, caught the act, and the experience was surreal. Every trick came to me in slow motion. Mary hung in mid-air, seemingly motionless like a black-and-white photo, while I had leisure time to search out her extended wrists and casually make the catch. What an extraordinary sensation it was. I only wish I could duplicate that experience "au nature."

# Chapter XXI

# Life As A Tourist

TIME TO SAY goodbye. We were excited over the proposed return trip up the East Coast and through the Suez Canal. Our usual tonnage of baggage was all loaded, and we need only thank our host and be outward bound. Once on board, we found our cabin quite luxurious. We had a port hole, a far cry from our previous passage where our cabin was so hot we slept topside under a ping pong table. Now, heading north, our first port of call was Zanzibar and with enough time to visit this legendary city. We hailed a pedicab, and after the usual tourist attractions, we entered an attractive lounge. I sidled up to the bar and, in what I hoped was a cosmopolitan manner, ordered a very dry martini. The bartender confessed he did not how to make this order. I casually pushed him aside, stepped behind the bar, and said, "Look and learn, my good man." Then proceeded to mix a very, very dry martini with two olives fished from their salad bowl. "You one very smart man, Boss," exclaimed the bartender. I tipped him lavishly.

Though this was still one of the Union Castle mail ships, by taking the canal route, our trip was more leisurely, making numerous port calls. Next was Mombasa, where we took advantage of a day's stop and hired a car to drive us into

Tanganyika for a night's lodging and a chance to see Kibo, the highest peak of Mt. Kilimanjaro. The ship had moved on so we reboarded at the next stop, Kismaayo. There was time enough in Aden, just before we entered the Red Sea, to take advantage of the duty-free port and purchase some more electronic devices and other useless souvenirs that still clutter up our closets and garage. As we entered the Suez Canal, we could see the dozens of huge ships, scuttled, by Nasser, lying half submerged in the effort to block shipping traffic through the canal during the dispute with Israel in 1956. We were able to ease past the remaining hulks and were rewarded with a two-day lay over to visit every seeable relic in Cairo. I realize this sounds like your neighbor's cocktail party where they hold you captive for an hour, showing photos and describing their first trip abroad. I can only hope you have a cocktail in hand. Don't spill it as we lurch our way past the pyramids on two hard-backed camels. Anyway, through the canal and into the Med (we world travelers call it the Med) and before the Strait of Messina, the volcanic island of Stromboli hove into view. It was big and black, smoldering around the edges, and the captain accommodated all on board by circling this movie setting before heading for Genoa. We got through the Strait of Gibraltar and into Southampton. We picked up our rolling stock and were in Switzerland, ready for another opening.

LEE STATH (MARILEES)

# Chapter XXII

# Lily Yokoi

OUT OF AFRICA and into the land of the Alps. This was the first time with the Knie Circus, though we were to return twice more during my career. This was the National Circus of Switzerland and one that drew the best performers from throughout the world. A tenting show, but we did enjoy many prolonged engagements in the larger cities, and the year passed smoothly; though I recall a conflict that developed between our act and Rolando, a Swedish hand balancer of some ability. His trump card was his wife, Lily Yokoi, a petite Japanese, and her "Golden Bicycle" act. She was good, and Rolando used every trick to overshadow us and usurp the Marilees from top billing. Opening night, in Zurich, he had salted the audience with the purchase of twenty-five tickets for young Swiss students who were instructed to applaud, shout, and generally induce the audience to follow suite for Lily Yokoi's performance. The cost of twenty-five tickets on opening night was considerable but well invested. The response was great for a great act. How could I begrudge him that coupe? As fate would have it, I had gone earlier to the local florist to have a large bouquet ordered and presented to Mary at the close of our act, which was customary. As I placed my order, the owner, learning I was from the circus, introduced himself and recommended a lovely floral display. I agreed and explained how and when it should be presented. He was most accommodating, and when I paid, he asked if I knew about Rolando's order and presentation. Quick as a snake, I seized the golden opportunity and said "Didn't Rolando get back to you on that? He decided a simple red rose would

be more impressive for this unassuming Japanese goddess." "I see, I see," he replied. "I can see his vision. Most artistic. And your bouquet?" "Oh, what the hell. Go ahead and double my order. You know how we Americans are."

"Opening night in Zurich with Circus Knie."

How I gloated and reveled at the single rose presentation, and how the audience stood and cheered after our successful act and the ring filled with flowers for Mary and the Flying Marilees. Take that, you Swedish swine.

# Chapter XXIII

# Charlie Chaplin's Contribution

HOWEVER, IT WASN'T always fun and games. Often, after the show, we would be called upon by our director, Herr Knie, to join in some festive evening. It meant dining out and being friendly to the many celebrities that called themselves "Circus Fans." They were always interesting, intelligent people, usually wealthy or prominent in some field of art or entertainment. I will not forget the evening we were invited out for dinner at Charlie Chaplin's villa in Vevey. It was situated lakeside and (as one might expect) as sumptuous and grand as any of the other millionaire mansions hugging the lakeshore. His wife, Oona, was gracious and beautiful. The children were so well behaved and polite and soon ushered off to bed with their nanny. We were introduced by the head of the household as the finest and most artistic aerialist to have ever graced his home. He gave us a brief tour of his estate, and I was pleased to see he had a room reserved simply for displaying movies. His library was extensive and contained an amazing variation of subjects. It seemed his taste covered a wide and varied spectrum. In the dining room, we took our seats at the massive antique table and were served by Oona, herself, though one could see servants lurking discreetly in the background. The food was exceptional and, as an ever-hungry artist, Texan, and survivor of the Great Depression era, I tried hard not to embarrass our representation as ambassadors of circus folk. When it came to afterdinner drinks, no reserve was required or expected. Rolf Knie, our employer, enjoyed having his artists drink, relax, and make fools of themselves. Just as long as we were in fighting form for the first performance the following day. Being in the presence of such a legendary star as Mr. Chaplin, I was careful to keep myself orderly and attentive to any stories or experiences he might relate. He was, at this time, collecting and assembling the events of his life for his autobiography. He mused over some of his more sensational episodes, contradicting much of the Hollywood interpretations and then, seeming to tire of the well-worn stories, turned and drew me near and in a somewhat conspiratorial voice asked if he could comment candidly on my act. I assured him I would be most appreciative of any suggestions or criticism he might have. He seemed a little hesitant and then eased into his opinion of the act. "You realize, I'm sure, you have one of the best aerial acts in the business today. You have, also, the most talented female aerialist I've seen performing plus the most charming and beautiful woman I've seen anywhere and, believe me, I'm a good judge in that field. I spent too many years in that melting pot called Hollywood." He took a critical sip of his cognac, held the glass to the light, paused, and gripped me by my shoulder and asked, "Do you realize how inadequate your music is?" I mulled over this question: music, background, a fanfare, some melody, a drum roll, and finish. What did that have to do with a flying trapeze act? "No

LEE STATH (MARILEES)

offense. I've been watching your act nightly since you've come to Vevey. Very enjoyable. But to be honest, the music hurts me. It could be so much better. It could be another partner in your act. It could make you great, no, I'm sorry. It could make you greater. With your permission, I could score new music for a fifteen-piece circus orchestra. I'm confident you'll find it supportive and an improvement." "Mr. Chaplin . . . ," I stammered. "Just call me Charlie." "Mr. Chaplin . . . Charles . . . Charlie, I'd be most honored." "Done," he cried.

We clinked or glasses, linked arms, and he said, "Kom, Wir trinking Brudershaft." And in that exhilarating moment, we were "brothers," at least in wine. We finished our drinks, and he seemed as genuinely pleased as I. We would have music from the master; and he could dabble, once again, in the fantasy of the circus; leave one more footprint of his genius behind.

"Charlie Chaplin and Lee drinking *Brudershaft* in Switzerland 1959."

And genius it was. I had previously been unaware of the circus band doing their best to keep up with our actions. When Chaplin's score arrived, was rehearsed and finally presented—I was genuinely stunned by the support and lift it gave the act. He had integrated, most generously and though subtly, his personal theme from his classic film *Limelight*. In the years following its introduction into our act and long after Charlie had passed on, we've worked many times under severe conditions. His gift has proven to be a crutch to help carry us through some very tedious times and often uninspired performances. Bless you, Charlie. You made a great act into an inspired act.

# Chapter XXIV

# Circus Schumann
# and Denmark

WITH THE STRAINS of Mr. Chaplin's composition buoying our spirits high, we moved on to Denmark for the 1960 season with Circus Schumann. What a jewel of an engagement. After a season of riding the rails, a new town every few days, then two shows, tear it all down, load it on the wagon, and move on to the next town, village, or city to do it again. Sounds tough and boring, and it was a physical challenge but never boring. Doing the act was rewarding enough. But when the contract came and we finally agreed on money, the prospect of working in Copenhagen, for Circus Schumann, in their permanent building for six months was such a delicious thought: You put up the rigging, 288 performances, and then one tear down. We could become "towners"; and so we did, renting a wonderful apartment with a real kitchen, a piano, separate room in which to eat and of course a bedroom that had its own toilet with running water. It may sound prosaic, but to us gypsies, this was a new and hedonistic pleasure. We bought ourselves a Lambretta scooter to run the five kilometers to and from our workplace.

Put-up day came, and I was anxious to get set up and practice as we had been off for four weeks and one's timing quickly needs rewinding. Oddly, Roger, our other flyer, had not yet arrived; but Mary picked up the slack and drove iron stakes like a man. The old building had no girders or rafters in the ceiling from which to hang our cables but was covered with a concrete dome one meter thick. We climbed up the outside of the building and onto the

"Look, sweetheart, there's the circus."

roof. I was shown several plugs that filled previously drilled holes. Still, a flying act rigging is fairly unique and dimensions precise. I was intrigued by how the available holes lined up perfectly for our rigging. We worked the day through, slipping the hang cables through, pulling the heavy apparatus fifteen meters off the sawdust floor. It was guyed out and ready for practice by midnight. Perhaps tomorrow, when we were fresher and cleaner. We went into the circus bar where Albert Schumann—the director, boss, or owner; a renowned horse trainer, performer, and artist from generations of Danish circus owners—greeted us. He was a tall lean man of thirty-five years, handsome, cultured, and fluent in five languages. He called us over for a Tuborg beer and said he was pleased to see that we had gotten the rigging set and looking forward to practice. "But where is your other flyer?" he asked. There was still a week before opening so no need to worry. Any day now. In came his stunning wife, Paulina.

LEE STATH (MARILEES)

Thick red hair fell on her shoulders, accenting a face so beautiful that I nearly ignored her low-cut dress that struggled to contain her other assets. She was Spanish, daughter to the world-famous clown, Charlie Rivals. He and his sons had won acclaim throughout the world. We were talking in English, and I commented on the good fortune of having found the existing holes in the roof nearly perfect for

"Paulina Schumann and Mary 1960."

our rigging. "Well, of course," Paulina said. "They were drilled by Alfredo Codona." I was stunned. Here was the name of the greatest flyer in circusdom, "Alfredo Codona."

I could not refer to him by his first name alone. He was ballet trained and self-taught with his brother, Lalo Codona, as his catcher. They were Americans of Mexican heritage, and my first introduction to this marvel was an old black-and-white 16-mm movie of him performing at the Winter Gardens in Berlin before the war. I was a novice; but the older, established flyers and catchers sat

"The Master; Alfredo Codona."

around picking out subtleties and minute movements during his tricks on film. His style was different from ours, and many a flyer struggled to copy the forgotten or lost method he had developed. Perhaps it only fit his particular body form. Like most good flyers, or "leapers," as some of the older generation called them, he was small: five feet seven inches at about 115 pounds. But what symmetry. His ballet slippers melted into the line of his legs with a pointing of toes that must have caused cramping in the night. The tricks he did, I can't describe. He did them all. He did tricks that hadn't been thought of, but more than that, he did them with grace, style, and finesse. I knew that he was dead. His death had been well before my introduction to this world of fantasy. "Whatever happened to him?" I asked "Ah, it's all too sad," Paulina said and left. "Yes," said Albert, "It was tragic. It actually began here in Copenhagen. You must understand that his wife, and really true love, was Lillian Lietzel, an aerialist of equal proficiency and success as was Alfredo." Mr. Schumann could call him Alfredo. "She did a solo single-trapeze number of such complexity and strength that her bookings were always in demand, and that brought her here to an elite night club not far from where our circus stands. This was before my time, but my father said that during the finish of her act, when she did those accelerated one arm swings, the hand loop broke and though she wasn't more than twenty-five feet from the floor, when she fell, it broke her neck and she died a short time later.

"God, that was tragic." I choked. "Yes, it was. But that wasn't the end of it." Albert continued, "Alfredo never really got over this loss. He continued flying, with the same intensity and success. It would be melodramatic to say he lost his love of flying when he lost Lillian. He was back in the States doing the triple somersault or "Saltomortal" as the Germans call it. Then the curse of flying caught him, and he tore out his shoulder. It dislocated, shredded the rotator cuff, and it was all over for him. So many flyers have their careers ended, productive years cut short, but you know all about this." Paulina had eased back into the conversation. "Tell them about Vera. That's the real sad part." Albert sighed resignedly. "Vera, Vera Bruce, was a good performer, but she felt it a coup to associate and be next to the greatest flyer in the world. They married and continued working on the show, but Alfredo was

"Codona's monument to his love, Lillian Lietzel. Note the broken hand loop at the base."

grounded and could only watch as other aerialists soared. He was not a jealous or envious man. He was willing to pass on his knowledge or pass on the torch to the next generation. But this was really not enough to mask his hurt, his frustration; his constant awareness of being a "Has Been". Vera didn't make things any easier." "No!" shouted Paulina. "She was the one. She only wanted his name, his reputation." "So it would seem," Albert agreed. "It wasn't long until she filed for divorce. It was in Los Angeles. 'Irreconcilable differences,' the decree stated. She had no idea how right she was. Alfredo shot her four times and then himself when they went to sign the papers in the lawyer's office. The radios interrupted their broadcasts, nationwide, to report the news. An "extra" edition went out from the press, telling of the loss of one of our greatest." A solemn sip from our beer stein, we bade all a goodnight and then rode silently back to our room to wonder about tomorrow's practice and our future in such an uncertain profession.

And one of those uncertainties was the continuing whereabouts of our other flyer. Once again, Roger did not honor his contract, and we were lacking the necessary third party.

Mr. Schumann contacted his agents; I contacted my sources. Between us, we came up with a likeable French chap, Andre Belfort, who was available and capable. He arrived

before opening, and with a few practices, we were ready. He could drop Mary's return bar and was able to do the big finish with her. The only fly in the ointment was that good old likeable Andre was not very handsome. One might say he was downright ugly. You might say so, but I wouldn't dare. So we opened in Copenhagen and the season began.

"Andre and Mary."

Shortly thereafter, Pater Schonig, the circus priest, contacted us and said he was coming for a visit. I met him at the airport and strapped his baggage on the back of our motor scooter, and off we went, his clerical garments flapping in the wind as we roared down the avenues with the amused onlookers turning to point out the sacred sight. We put him up in our apartment where he slept on our couch. Next morning, with my coffee espresso and Mary's exotic omelet, he said it was the highlight of his visits. Hail Mary full of grace.

## Chapter XXV

# King Frederick's Salute

**W**ITH LIFE AT a new seemingly normal pace, I wanted to take advantage of our leisure and proximity to the sea. My dream of retiring someday and living aboard our yacht and sailing to far-off islands, whose very names elicit visions of excitement and adventure, was whetted by books of previous yachtsmen and their hazardous passages. So it was down to the sea to Borghman's yacht basin. What a pleasant and likeable old man he was. Surrounded in his boat yard with various length wooden craft, most being overhauled and readied for the oncoming summer, I confided my passion and desire for a boat of my own. I must have touched some nerve of his own and a vision of a long passage through unfamiliar waters. Instead of any high-pressure sales talk, he suggested I lease one of his available boats, sail it for the season, and he would buy it back when our circus engagement was done. That seemed reasonable. What would I do with a sailboat, tied up in Denmark, when we took off for Switzerland or, perhaps, Swaziland? So this old mariner pointed out this lovely Folksboat, a lap strake sloop sitting propped up on the ways. She had just been hauled out, scraped, and painted. He put on a full set of sails and told me to enjoy. Mary put her fear of the water aside. I was the captain and I made her first mate.

Summertime in Denmark with me at the helm. We made many a wild, imaginary passage through uncharted seas, touching foreign ports (we did make the short run across to Sweden), reefing

"Close hauled on our way to Sweden."

down in one short squall, and just getting back in time for the night show looking like drowned rats.

I feel the high point of my life at sea was when King Frederick IX of Denmark saluted us. And why not? I had lashed an American flag to our mast top and one sunny day, as we tacked through the harbor, we passed astern of the king's royal yacht, tied to the wharf and with the royal flag flying. We passed close by; and as I pointed out to Mary this beauty of a yacht, I saw the seaman, standing watch on the stern, jerk his head around and disappear into the cabin. In a moment, he dashed back and quickly lowered the Danish royal flag as we foamed by. The king of Denmark was saluting our tiny sloop and our flag. But our flag was lashed securely to the topmast, and I could only wave our respects and hope I had not created an international incident.

# Chapter XXVI

# Sue Me

WITH THE SEASON just reaching the halfway point, Mr. Schumann brought in an entire Russian magic show to add some variety to the circus performance. It was a huge production and had at least fifty new personnel. With such an added expense, he was obliged to let half of the circus artists go. Mary and I had never been satisfied with our French flyer, so it was no surprise when Schumann terminated our contract. We took down our rigging and were about to leave when Larry Griswold, that world-class comedy, trampoline act, and best friend, took me aside and said the show couldn't do that. "Get a lawyer and fight this thing." I couldn't see much promise in fighting a circus owner on his own turf, but I engaged a lawyer nevertheless and took Mr. Schumann, a Danish citizen, to a Danish judge. In short, the judge argued that if Mr. Schumann was dissatisfied with the act, why did he keep it for three months? "Apparently, you were satisfied for three months. Why should you now become dissatisfied at this late date?" Therefore, he was obliged to pay us for the remainder of the season as stated in the contract. Three months pay and we were free to go. When we exited the judge's chambers, Mr. Schumann took me by the hand and said, "Well done, Lee."

We hung around a week to catch the new, Russian magic show. Admittedly, it was interesting and quite a novelty. Many of the tricks involved an artist disappearing on stage. Truly mystifying. A young man or girl (there were many) would be sealed inside a trunk, tied hand and foot, and padlocked before being raised into the air, but when lowered and opened, it was empty. That was to be expected, a false bottom probably; but when the same young artist materialized up in the second balcony, waving, it was stunning. How could they do it? I was awestruck until the day I happened backstage and saw a score of identical twins. There was a set for each trick. Only a state-owned circus, like the Russians, could afford such a luxury as that. But what happens after the show? Even the Soviets couldn't keep a cast of thirty odd performers locked in a basement for three months. Enter the gentlemen in the dark suits. They would accompany a twin, one at a time, for a tour of the town, a restaurant, a movie, or museum; but no towner ever saw two at a time. That has been over fifty years ago, I hope my divulging those secrets will not place a black mark against my name the next time we visit Russia.

Perhaps I shouldn't worry. During that same season, there was a Polish teeter board act, eight strong and firmly from the Soviet Bloc. I had a red pullover that I happened to wear on this coolish spring day. When we arrived at the show, the entire troupe grabbed and hugged me crying, "Comrade! Comrade!" How was I to know it was the festive Russian "May Day"? They were all wearing red. It would seem that I was one of them. Perhaps we will still be welcome.

# Chapter XXVII

# The German Invasion

WE TOOK OUR ill-gotten settlement money from the Schumann contract and bought a new Opel Caravan (a station wagon of sorts) laid an air mattress in the back, and made our first foray into Spain. Winter in Alicante was heaven. I knew we had the contract with Krone in Germany come spring, and once again, we needed a flyer. Still, with warm sunshine, ripe figs for the taking, I found myself lulled into a Manana mood. How Herr Sembach, the owner and director of Circus Krone found us, I can't fathom. But there was a long distance phone call from Munich. One cannot imagine the primitive long distance phone complications of the early '60s and in Spain and speaking German. With a failure to communicate satisfactorily, I finally shouted, in frustration, "We'll be in Munich day after tomorrow." And so we were.

Face to face with the stern possessor of our signed contract, I had to confess that we could not fulfill that promise. We had no flyer. "Das macht nicht!" shouted Herr Sembach. "You still have Miss Marilees, nicht wahr?" Yes, Mary was working, but I suspect Herr Sembach's daughter, Christel, liked Mary as much as I did. "I'll find you a flyer!" vowed "Der Meister," and so he did.

We settled into the local Gasthaus on the outskirts of Munich where Herr Sembach introduced us to Gerhardt, a young, typical German lad, twenty years or so but professing to have some knowledge of flying. *We'll see about that*, I thought. Arrangements were made by the director, and a place to hang our rigging for practice was made. He gave us three weeks. He would then come and see if it was "Krone" worthy. Our practice site was near our lodgings and turned out to be old quarters for the Nazi SS troops. The barred windows still held the iron swastika symbols, but the roof had been bombed and left gaping holes to the outside blizzards. We found steel girders intact and were able to hang our rigging. Practice was torture. We hoped for a lull in the storm, but this was Bavarian winter, and there was no lull. Swathed in sweaters, jackets and gloves, teeth clenched, we climbed the icy ladder. We stripped only long enough to swing out and try to fly. Snow blew in through the jagged, gashed ceiling; and with hands numb, muscles brittle, we tried to make a new act out of an unknown. In all fairness, Gerhardt did his best. I was pained to ask Mary to try another trick under those conditions. Each practice was an ordeal and full of risk.

Nights at the Gasthaus were only slightly better. Our room was so chilled that the radiators were colder than we were. I went down to the proprietors' to complain and was met at the door by a fat man in an undershirt. "So what's your problem?" he asked.

The weeks ached by, but there was some hope as Gerhardt was progressing and showed real keenness. The day of reckoning arrived. Herr Sembach and his entourage entered our igloo. They were dressed warmly in furs and mufflers. They stood by the net and said, "Show me!" We struggled up and we struggled through managing to catch everything. "Ja! That's OK." and they were gone.

Back at the Gasthaus, we wanted to celebrate this accomplishment. With rounds of schnapps, we toasted Gerhardt, pounding his back and lauding his efforts and achievements. In a short three weeks, he had become a flyer, a flyer of Sembach's acceptance. Next morning, as we went downstairs to breakfast with our new flyer, I was told by the Wirt that our friend, Gerhardt, had checked out very early. We never heard another word or explanation of his disappearance. Short of an alien abduction, I can only guess that he was too awed at the challenge of working for Herr Sembach, a near clone of Der Fuhrer.

"The fearful image of Carl Krone."

# Chapter XXVIII

# What Next?

UNDER THE CIRCUMSTANCES, Christmas in Bavaria seemed too bleak. We agreed that the familiarity of Paris might lighten our spirits. It wasn't a long jump and the snow eased off as we entered France. Almost like coming home and when we arrived at the Cirque d'hiver, we were welcomed by old friends and keen rivals, the Flying Palacios.

Here we were, in Paris, coming to watch you and your family for the big Christmas engagement. Still a week before opening so we could relax and perhaps swing on their rigging to try and keep that evaporating touch. We were at the Artist's Café when Medini, our Italian agent, burst in and grabbed me in a typical Italian embrace and shouted, "Thank, God, you're here." *Damn*, I thought, *we're here because we blew the season in Germany*, and he must have known that. "Cognac for the table," he ordered; and then pulling close to us, he whispered, "I need your act for Cirque Medrano, across town." I knew the Medrano Circus. It was an old building that had been declared a National Monument. The dressing rooms were dusty, drafty, and rat infested, yet if the money was right . . ." We'd love to help, but, as you know, we haven't got a flyer." I couldn't believe what Lalo said. Since we were competitors and always fighting for the same contracts, why would he suggest, "My little brother, Roberto, could help you out." So there in the "Café des Artists," we all tossed down our cognac, toasting another version of the Flying Marilees.

Yes, we shared some good times. Remember Paris, during that Christmas season? After the last show, I couldn't wait to see you back at the hotel to hear if you had caught your triple and gloat if we had caught ours. Remember that hotel on Rue Lepic? That firetrap of five stories? We shared the same floor. For that matter, we shared the same toilet and bath. It was down the hall at the far end, and how we competed for its use and the tepid water from that eccentric plumbing.

"Rue Lepic in Pigalle."

We were all tired of cold brie and Beaujolais. So Mary put a suitcase on the bidet, set our tiny primus stove precariously on top and voila! We had a kitchen. You promised a culinary treat unrivaled in the French restaurants and true to your promise and Mexican heritage, you produced chili rellenos that brought tears to my eyes, both then and now.

We passed many a night of eating, drinking, and boasting of tricks performed, tricks caught, and tricks only imagined, there in that shabby Hotel Prima in Pigalle. Yet you were quiet and noncommittal the night we came back from our night show and we rushed down to the bar to tell you that the Russian State Circus was opening at the Palais d' Sports and the entire troupe of performers had come to our circus. Here were the elite acrobats, clowns, and State-trained artists from Russia. The greatest they could combine and send forth for the world to see. I was intimidated as they filled a complete section of our venerable antique circus. Admittedly, our show was only mediocre, but they sat politely and silently as it drug on. At intermission, I was certain they would leave; but as we erected the net for our act, I was surprised to see them retake their seats. "Look who's coming back for seconds" I muttered to the prop boss as we tightened the net. "Yeah," he replied, "but look who their ushers are." Sure enough, intermingled among the group were four dark—suited gray tie types that showed more interest in their Russian wards than they did the show. And rightfully so, I later learned. These somber figures were not circus trained but a spinoff of the KGB. Russian performers, be they circus, ballet, orchestral, or opera, all had their small posse of "keepers" that accompanied them on any outside venture. Whether to the restaurant, a cinema, a museum, or a show like ours, their silent shadows were always present. When I say silent, I mean they were always part of our conversations, even if only as interested eavesdroppers. But for this, they were highly qualified, each one speaking, or better yet, understanding four or five languages.

Now seated, the lights dimmed, and the Flying Marilees were announced. A single spotlight caught us in mid-ring. Mary had chosen a flesh-colored costume, weighted with hand-sewn sequins and rhinestones set in a pattern that concealed little but accentuated much. I had watched her sewing these tiny bits of shiny glitter with painstaking care and endless patience. Now it was fulfilled. It was worth her months of tedious dedication. She was glorified. As the first burst of limelight drenched our figures in the dark, circus ring, an audible, muffled gasp flowed in from the crowd. From only a short distance, she appeared nude. This perfectly sculpted body of sensuality seemed stark naked yet clothed in shimmering glitter. All this and crowned with golden soft flowing blonde hair that covered her shoulders and back. What a tremendous entrance, but could she sing?

We climbed the rigging; and, I'll only say, we performed well. It was a good act; it was an inspired act. We missed nothing; and as Mary returned to the pedestal board from her closing trick, the entire Russian contingent, including the four stooges, stood as one. Out of their seats and on their feet applauding, shouting, cheering, "Brava! Brava!" How we loved the Russians back in 1960.

"Mary: Sex goddess."

Back at the hotel bar, I related all this to Lalo with unrestrained enthusiasm. I was in high spirits. It was our big night. He sipped his wine slowly, stood up, adjusting his tailored shirt into his tailored trousers, and said, "I caught my triple tonight." He kissed Mary's hand, said good night, walked to the door, turned for a brief moment, and looked at me with an expression of envy, hate, or admiration. It was so fleeting, I was never sure.

LEE STATH (MARILEES)

Many years earlier, this Mexican flying act had settled up with Ringling Brothers and accepted the acreage of the old winter quarters in lieu of money owed them by the show. What a coup. Those bare acres, which they turned into a trailer park, were home for many a nomadic artist on their way to or from some exotic engagement. As time passed, land values increased; and there, in the heart of town, stands this defiant circus family, clutching firmly to a gold mine. Damn you, Lalo Palacio, We were always competitors. I was sure our act was better than yours. With Mary as our feature attraction, I felt we were slightly, yes, only slightly better than the Flying Palacios. Lalo was graceful, but so was Mary. Lalo did big tricks, but so did Mary. What was the difference? What tipped the scales in our favor? She was beautiful and she was sexy. Ability, beauty, and sex, how could one compete against that? Still, Lalo, you had that choice piece of property in the heart of Sarasota. What were you lacking? Why did you kill yourself that cold, wet night in Lille, France? I know we were never close, but Mary told me how you confided in her and wept in her arms that evening we partied in a small bistro in Pigalle. She tried to share your pain. I could not. Was he worth that great sacrifice?

Another hectic, prosperous, exciting year ended. One last riotous New Years party. We left Paris and returned to America. Our only excess baggage was the recurring nightmare of searching for a flyer. Like a homing pigeon, we wound our way back to Sarasota to lick our wounds, greet old friends, and search for a flyer. Wintertime here but not the likes of Bavaria. There was always a rigging up on Danny's spacious trailer park where we had settled. There would be no problem keeping in shape; finding a flyer was. Then came the tragic news of Mike Malko's sudden death. He had still been young, a robust catcher, but always a bit overweight. His heart gave up. The tragic news filtered through the park, but the news struck me like the chord of some beautiful hymn. I could scarcely conceal my joy. Mike Malko was Tony Steele's catcher; and who, you might ask, was Tony Steele?

"Tony Steele."

Only the best flyer in the business in the last four decades. Tony had finally resurrected the triple salto after so many years of dormancy. In fact, few people, in our generation, could boast of ever having seen one. Tony was free and Tony would need a new catcher, only one obstacle. Tony was in the army stationed somewhere in Germany. Enter the sinister and enigmatic Herr Butz, front man for the state-sponsored German circus touring the world on a goodwill mission. They needed some sensational aerial act for their Far East engagement. I could give them that. First, they had to get Tony out of the army. I don't want to know how it was achieved but in a few short weeks, Tony and his wife Lily met us in New York for the start of a dream contract.

Once there, we picked up our tickets at the Air France office. I was puzzled by, what seemed to me, the devious route: New York to Hamburg to Alaska and finally Tokyo.

This was not my first experience of air travel, but in the sixteen years gone by, I had developed a fear of flying, quite a phobia for a trapeze artist. Our tickets put us in the rear section of this beautiful white flying machine. My window seat was wasted. I sat, hunched down, eyes clenched shut, all the way across the Atlantic. How I longed for the good old days when we sailed leisurely aboard the great ocean liners. That would mean a week to cross the Atlantic. There were soft nights with a fire flecked, fluorescent wake trailing astern. We would make smooth progress with fantastic food, games, dances, and the chance to stretch out and sleep the night through. But now air borne, only a mere six hours, and we were landing in Hamburg. I was relieved and delighted at the simplicity of such travel. Flying the Great Circle over the Pole, and we would be in Tokyo tomorrow.

We had time for a bit of fresh air and some German beer while they refueled Air France's pride, the flagship "Chateau de Versailles." I was so elated over our successful conquest of the Atlantic that I decided to film our take off. Realize this was in the early sixties, and I had a small, 8-mm Bolex movie camera. Video was still a thing to come. As our seating was well aft, in the tail section, I had a good view of the tarmac, the massive port wing, and both of its thundering, diesel engines. In a moment, we were racing down the runway; and with my camera, pressed close to the window, the ground tore through my view finder. What a rush! Like an experienced camera man, I panned from right to left, following the path of the catapulting giant tandem wheels. CATAPULTING GIANT TANDEM WHEELS? For that brief split second, before catastrophe, I wondered if the wheels were jettisoned on takeoff; but then I viewed the wing dip slowly down and strike fire on the concrete like an old-fashioned phosphorous match on sand paper. It was only then, at that moment, that the realization struck me. I dropped my camera and tucked tight in a fetal position and waited to die. Oh, how slowly time goes when you are waiting to die. The roar of the diesel engines was replaced with a low rumbling sound accompanied with an ear—piercing screeching as the aluminum fuselage tore itself apart on the concrete. Then a lull; the screeching stopped; the rumbling continued; and now we began to lurch, bounce, and tear across the soft earth of some farmer's field like a gigantic plow gone berserk. The turbulence eased, another lurch and jolt, and we stopped. There was silence. Eerie silence. I saw a sliver of sky open just in front of our section. The first sound or motion I detected was the Japanese hostess, a petite, ceremonially dressed girl who made a lasting impression on me when she lifted her long brocaded skirt up around her hips and shouted, "Follow me." Normally, one exits these airliners by descending a long flight of portable stairs. Now, with the plane broken in three sections and the landing gear stripped away, we found ourselves at ground level. We need only slip through the torn opening and sprint for safety.

I was quickly out of my seat belt and looking frantically for

"Holy Smoke! Air France has landed."

LEE STATH (MARILEES)

Mary. As usual, she had anticipated the threat of disaster and released her belt immediately. I finally found her under a seat, three rows ahead. She was alive. I was alive. We might just get out of this twisted wreck alive. We filled out in an orderly manner of panic and rejoiced at being outside, alive and uninjured. Until Mary screamed, "My purse! Get my purse!" Like any stunned, terror-stricken husband, I turned and reentered the now burning wreckage. I got the damn purse and rejoined the survivors sprinting away at what we thought was a safe distance. We turned and looked back at our escaped tomb. It was lying flat in the field; the forward section was broken away at the front of the wings. The main part of the fuselage was lying limp, and just behind this was our tail section. This beautiful white graceful machine was now engulfed in billowing black-and-gray columns of smoke. She was dead. We were alive.

In the inevitable investigation that always follows, it was determined that the wheels locked on takeoff, causing them to sheer off at near takeoff speed. The good news was that the freshly filled fuel tanks left no room for

"Please keep your seat belts fastened until after we've crashed."

the volatile gas to collect. Consequently, we had a slow burning plane from which to flee. An interesting side light was seeing the Air France crew, with ladders propped against the flaming wreckage, diligently and casually, painting out the "Air France" lettering on the fuselage.

We and the walking wounded, were quickly ushered into various transports and taken to a nearby hotel. Before our ill-fated takeoff, we were issued soft Oriental slippers that would have been ideal for the long tedious flight but ill-suited for running through broken glass, flaming debris, and runway rubble. But once in the hotel, the powers

Noch rauchten die Trümmer, als der Name der Fluggesellschaft übertüncht wurde. Die Gesellschaft fürchtet um ihren guten Ruf.

"French artists at work."

that be magically produced a cornucopia of footwear for his and hers. Women, who moments before were sobbing, praying, and crossing themselves in gratitude for life, now were elbowing, pushing, and grasping at the stylish French footwear to replace some of the less-than-fashionable shoes left behind. An Air France associate worked his way through the passengers, listing items lost in the crash. Purses were found, lost cash reimbursed, souvenirs and trinkets were retrieved, but my movie camera was never returned. Air France replaced it with a far superior model. I feel certain that my camera was found and kept, and the film reviewed with the possibility of seeing something of interest or technically disclosing. Either way, I didn't want to review that scene ever again.

Our partner, Tony Steele, could not agree more. We sat together on the spiral marble staircase of our hotel, accepting the endless shots of schnapps proffered to us courtesy of Air France. We were both grateful to be alive and uninjured. We still had our contract in Tokyo, and I was eager to get on with it. Tony, on the other hand, said he would never get on an airplane again. He was looking forward to a long passage back to America on a slow freighter. Mary and I had other plans for him, more schnapps. Morning came; and, though he was oblivious to it, we put Tony on board a very fast Air France jet bound for Tokyo.

# Chapter XXIX

# Marilees In Wonderland

FORGET YOUR WORLD atlas. It was still a puzzle to me, but we were flying due north over the "top of the world," stopping in Anchorage to refuel and long enough for Tony and me to get out, kick the tires, and make other inexperienced checks of the aircraft before the final leg to Tokyo.

What a reception we received on arrival. There were dignitaries, garlands of flowers, and a stretch limo that shunted us quickly to our hotel. I was tempted to cry out "Wait a minute, fellows. We haven't even caught a trick yet." But that was pretty much what the show was like. I'm still at a loss as to what was behind this German goodwill tour. Money was of no concern. All hotel, taxis, air transportation, restaurants, and incidental expenses were paid. Our salary alone made me suspicious. I wondered if all we had to do was a flying act.

"The Marilees have arrived."

One touching note: our first practice in the Korakuen Ice Palace. In all honesty, Tony and I had never worked together. He had been in the army two years. Could he still do it? Late at night, after we had hung the rigging, we went up to see. A goodly number of the artists were sequestered in the dimly lit arena. We made a few swings, did a couple of simple tricks, and I said, "Let's see what it looks like." I had hung for a lot but never caught a triple. I could sense Tony's nervousness, but he put up the top raise and stepped off. So much has happened in the years since then, a lot of success and a lot of failures, some love and some hate. Now looking up in the scarce light and seeing this tiny balled-up missile spinning in space, I felt a witness of something great. Admittedly, in the scheme of life, it was meaningless, but to me, it was one of my high points. We missed the trick and the next one and another. But on the fourth try, I snagged it. The few observers erupted. Tony came down into the net and lay there sobbing. I climbed down and embraced him, reassuring him he was back home again. Such is the relationship between flyer and catcher.

# Chapter XXX

# Mary Again

THAT WAS ONE of the factors that made the marriage of Mary and me such an unyielding bond of love and trust. I held her in my hands, literally, for sixty years. Interesting how two such dissimilar upbringings could spawn such a deep love and sometimes tumultuous relationship. She would reminisce of her childhood, growing up in a mansion like home with acres of land and a huge barn with heaters, hay, and stalls where they kept the elephants and lions. Outside there was a special plot where the bears would burrow and hibernate for the winter. Happy birthday! What did Mary get from her dad? Not a pony, as the ultimate gift for a kid, but a baby elephant was Mary's present from her dad.

Contrast that with my parents tiny rented house alongside the railroad tracks and a lawn full of stickers and

"Mary's birthday present."

dead grass: her father, a successful circus owner; my dad, a crippled vet left over from the first World War; and my devoted, hardworking Irish mother trying to supplement his meager $30 monthly pension. Mary and I made a great team.

# Chapter XXXI

# An American In Japan

OUR CONTRACT STRESSED that we were to maintain a high level of decorum, attending all diplomatic functions, representing the German government in the best manner and with the highest standards. We, personally, intended to show our act to the best of our ability; and our conduct was usually acceptable. As for the near nightly invitations to the various government functions, we quickly learned they consisted of very formal introductions, high praise of our nation (Germany), vast arrays of local cuisine brought forth endlessly, and as much alcohol as the table, hosts, and guests could support. There was much singing, dancing, and improper advances made toward all the attractive girls and a few of the startled men. This was diplomacy at its highest level. We learned early to line our stomachs with a few shots of heavy cream or a spoon of butter before being feted by these well-meaning, party-hungry hosts. I think we upheld the German honor well.

Transportation, always a headache for an act on the road, was supplied and paid for. Country to country was by chartered plane. This was not always a good thing. With all the circus performers, our wardrobe trunks and personal belongings, plus all the circus equipment (our pig iron steel tubing, net, cables, and pulley blocks making up a high percentage of the gross weight) were placing a maximum burden on some of the older airplanes. On one such trip to Shanghai, we lumbered down the runway, aborted the takeoff and were assigned a longer runway. This too proved inadequate. So with typical oriental ingenuity, we all were asked to disembark. A crew of coolies entered and removed all the seating and other unessential items. Hostesses, and any other person not necessary to the actual flying of the craft were grounded. Even our director and the ringmaster were told to join us later. I was tempted to sacrifice my squatting place but was told to hold on to the person next to me, and so we staggered into the air just short of the end of the runway. I'm sure I heard, above the roar of four overtaxed engines, the pilot, and copilot shouting "Banzai!" There were no peanuts or orange juice served on that flight.

When we landed, we were once again met by high dignitaries; flowers hung round our sweaty necks, and photos taken with each official standing among us. "Circus Berlin" had arrived.

The press was always eager for an interview, and I was always obliging. "You are the first to catch the triple in Japan. Yes? Yes, that was true. "This is your first trip to our land. Yes?" Well, no. But I shouldn't have elaborated. After more than fifteen years, I didn't realize they were still so sensitive over their defeat. The war was done and forgotten so I shouldn't have gone into detail about my first visit to their Imperial Shores back in 1944. Our submarine had slipped in on the surface, near a deserted beach, on a dark, moonless night. A couple of lads and myself implored the skipper to let us swim ashore and "invade" Japan. He must have thought it had some humorous merit, but he stated firmly, "I'm leaving in one hour with or without you fools." We wasted no time. Once ashore, we threw a few handfuls of sand in the air and hurried right back. That was it. No harm done. and I thought it would make good print. The press thought otherwise. This boast on my part may have evoked memories of the incident when a US submarine moved into another shallow inlet and lay submerged for six hours, waiting patiently with the train schedule sitting on the skippers chart table. At the appointed time, a periscope eased slowly to the surface; and as the train approached the wooden trestle, spanning the far end of the inlet, a single torpedo, fired a thousand yards away, shattered the structure and brought it down with the train tumbling into the void. On her return to the base, hers was the only sub who proudly carried a train engine, painted on the conning tower, alongside the other ships she had sunk.

There were other errors in this foreign land. Did you know that one should soap and scrub BEFORE you enter the hot mineral baths? I didn't. Not until the kimono-clad geisha chastised and led me back to the shower. Damn, uncouth Americans!

Despite my blunderings, the show was well received and after the customary ceremonies, we were ushered into a large hotel. Strong drink was provided, and we were seated in a sumptuous dining hall. There were more waiters attending us than there were show people, and we had a big show. Some unknown hors d'oeuvres were offered and greedily accepted, as was the sake (rice wine). Now that we were softened up, they brought in the piece de resistance,

LEE STATH (MARILEES)

Peking duck! What a great display and so dramatically presented. A half-dozen waiters entered, each carrying a single tray laden with that legendary golden brown duck surrounded, artfully, with greenery. Each fragrant tray was taken to each guest and proudly displayed. "Yes, yes!" my teased palate screamed out, but no, no! Just as we expected these morsels to be served, they were whisked quickly back into the kitchen. We all sat in stunned silence as more sake was served. A poor substitute. It was then, however, I saw through their fiendish scheme. It was some form of Chinese torture, and I was more than willing to tell them where the treasure was buried or any state secrets I didn't know. But just before I could embarrass myself with any audible whimpering, they once again returned. Now the ducks had been skinned; and the crisp brown succulent pieces were rolled into a decorative shape, and the moist meat was stuffed inside, and this was only the beginning. I don't remember who started it, but our entire company began applauding. The staff, waiters, and cooks bowed in acknowledgment but remained inscrutable.

# Chapter XXXII

# Viet Nam Before Viet Nam

"**W**ERE YOU IN Nam?" I have had many Viet Nam veterans ask me that; and, yes, I was there. I rarely elaborate and explain that I was there before the Americans were sent in back in 1964. That doesn't mean we didn't see some action as far back as 1961. It was in Saigon; and our circus troupe was being chauffeured to our hotel, having just arrived at the airport, when a single Viet Cong fighter plane came in low, strafing and bombing the royal palace. Only minor damage was done as it was merely a show of strength. But we thought it great fun picking up pieces of smoldering, bomb fragments, and shrapnel. No one suspected what was yet to come.

Despite the late-evening shows, after our shower, we would stroll down to the waterfront and watch the cargo ships unload endless streams of helicopters swathed in cocoonlike wrappings. What does it all mean? Not to worry. There was a great, French restaurant we frequented. The stuffed crab au gratin was reason enough to visit Saigon. Now, in the midst of our meal and even before dessert, a window was smashed, and a hand grenade bounced onto our table. I am sorry to admit that I sat stunned; but Edgar Heltano, the shows juggler, snatched it up and heaved it back out the shattered window. The explosion broke the remaining windows, but no one was injured, not even by flying glass. Admittedly, we were all pretty shaken, but the majority of the patrons seemed almost indifferent. We too had become used to the distant rumble of heavy guns and bombs, but this was getting too close. Time to move on, and we almost didn't make that.

It was near our last week in Saigon when, during the night show, Chimaro, the sway pole artist, pushed the pole past its limit and it snapped. Set too near the audience, it fell among the spectators, perhaps good fortune for Chimaro but unfortunate for one individual who was smashed under the steel poles' weight and was killed in his seat. Chimaro walked away with a broken arm and minor contusions. But now our departure for Bangkok was put on permanent hold. The show was being held responsible, and a lawsuit was issued. Not surprisingly, the shows' "patch" or fixer was left behind to fix things, and the show made the Bangkok opening.

Bangkok, a city not to be forgotten. *Anna and the King of Siam* gives one only a casual glimpse of the splendor. Here, for us, there was nothing but beauty in the endless stretch of temples, gardens, restaurants, and food

"The King of Siam's Royal Barge."

booths. Yes—we did do a special performance for the King of Siam.

Things were not as grand for our Korean tour. We had the misfortune of arriving just after the May 16 coup. American troupes were ever present. This was somewhat reassuring, and we benefited from the Shangri-la of the American PX. We made a depressing visit, on the outskirts of Seoul, to a shambled village along the river. Chung was the grim name of this grim accumulation of shacks and shanties. It seemed nearly half the citizens or refugees were crippled. Some were dragging their twisted limbs through the filth and garbage. There but for the grace of God . . . we worked our way up as far as Inchon and inched our way up to the thirty-eighth parallel to peak over at the North Korean side. The North Koreans peered back over the barbed wire that kept the two enemies from hostilities, at least for the moment. Somewhat spoiled by our usual royal treatment, we accepted, with commendable humility, the humble accommodations sometimes presented. We spent several weeks in grass huts with dirt floors, and we were advised to brush our teeth using 7-Up rather than the contaminated local water. One kindly American evangelist, on seeing Mary and I wandering the desolate streets, gave us a note to be given the local mission reading, "Give these folks a hot meal." It was time to dress a bit neater and stop looking like the natives.

Not the case when we entertained in the Philippines. We were sequestered in the world's largest indoor arena (at that time), the Araneta Coliseum. We were not the last Americans to thrill the Philippine audiences. There was that memorable— Thrilla in Manila in 1975 when Muhammad Ali met Joe Frasier.

The building had hotel-style suites for the performers. Breakfast, lunch, and dinner were served whenever we were in the mood. Though the arena was situated some miles from Manila, we had no need to venture into the city. We lazed poolside in the sun, nibbling fresh papayas with lime juice. Orange juice and mangos were

"The massive Araneta Coliseum in Manilla."

brought at our bidding. This was interrupted only once when Mr. Araneta had us out to his mansion for dinner. First he took us out to his own arena where he bred and tested some of his prized fighting cocks. That was great sport in the islands. In his house, he was divided over his pride of the massive unique (at these times) stereo system or his four grotesquely overweight children. It was a status of great wealth to be overfed. We did quite well ourselves at his dining table.

After that glorious month in Manila, we had a one-night stand at Naha in Okinawa. It was to be a show for the American Forces stationed there; and General Chiang Kai-Shek, the Chinese Nationalist leader, was to be there. On a tiny island in the Pacific Ocean, I guess it was no wonder that the wind blew at such force. The stage was swept clean of any and all colorful decorations. All the acts struggled through, but I felt it would be impossible for us to perform. I was partly correct. The show went on, but when we tried to do a trick, our swing was stopped dead; and we were left hanging like dirty laundry. The troops didn't seem to mind. Mary was scantily dressed.

Our final fascinating tour of the Far East was at the contentious island of Formosa. Our primary base was in Taipei, and for a change, we traveled by rail as far south as Kaohsiung. This was rail travel to which one could become addicted. The seats were luxurious; and hot tea was endlessly served, accompanied with damp hot towels for our weary eyes and necks.

Most of our performances were in outdoor areas hastily put up in some vast field where they erected temporary bamboo fences. This proved to be a futile exercise in security as the thousands of eager patrons soon trampled them down, and the audience flowed in and around the performers. I've always been fearful of someone walking beneath the net during a trick. If we were to miss, someone could be killed, and it could be one of us. Under these uncontrollable situations, it meant giving up or not missing a trick. Somewhat foolhardy, I chose to keep it in the air and be sure not to miss. Finishing our act, we normally came down with some spectacular dive into the net, not before these avid patrons. We were forced to climb down and accept their "up close and personal" congratulations. Even our bamboo-erected

"It's show time in Korea."

LEE STATH (MARILEES)

dressing rooms were not safe. These people wanted to see the "whole show."

After each hectic performance, our hotels were truly a sanctuary. With hot thermal baths, soft music, and clean clothes, we were almost reluctant to wander outside in search of another eating experience. Yet it was always well worth the effort, never a disappointment. It was then I realized that I had never really eaten Chinese food before.

With late shows, we had time to wander the cities and see the exotic lifestyle. Mary found a dimly lit establishment where we found an Aladdin's treasures up for sale. We couldn't refuse the huge mahogany tea table with four matching stools and with such intricate carving. The table's four-inch deep carving told of some epic Chinese battle amid a forest of shrubs and trees with samurai warriors on horseback and afoot. Nearby was a matching cedar chest, five feet in length, two and half feet in depth and with the same intricate motif. It would be perfect for Mary's furs when we settled down somewhere in the future. For days, we returned to the shop to haggle over the price. In the end, we agreed we had to have them. We bought it all and had it shipped to my mother's house back in Kansas. It was some months later that we received a letter saying that the freighter, carrying our goods, had ran aground and sank off the coast of Catalina, all the way across the Pacific and almost safe at home. We shrugged it off and were grateful, at least, that we hadn't been aboard. Then sometime later, my mother wrote that the chest and table had arrived. The ship had been salvaged, and we were one of the happy winners. It was many years later before we ever got to Kansas and the treasures were still in their original crates. The sets sit now in our Texas living room. The glass top for the table was shattered; and the surface, though still pristine, has a noticeable warp. Still, the beauty and the memories remain. With that, our tour of the Far East was ended. We were hustled over to Hong Kong where we boarded the P & O liner, SS *Chusan*, bound for Hawaii.

LEE STATH (MARILEES)

# Chapter XXXIII

# Who Says You Can't Go Home?

HONOLULU, IN 1962, was a far cry from what I remembered eighteen years previously. I believe the biggest change for me was having a wife, someone close with which to share this beautiful island. Only one day before we sailed for home, so we tried to do as much as possible in that short time span. I rented a red convertible; and with the top down, I must have, surely, given some observant TV writers the idea for Magnum PI. Sitting in the tropical sun, I spun the wheels; and we toured the Island, ate the food, and did all the things visiting tourists do.

"Lee in the Islands while Magnum PI
was still in grade school."

Even so, at the end of the day and the Far East tour, I was more at ease to be aboard a large ship in open waters again. Next stop; Seattle and the 1962 Seattle World's Fair.

With all the complaining I've done about one-day stands, wrestling rigging up and down—the endless journeys made, here we were, another day in paradise, better yet, six months of it. The German good-will tour had picked this plum, and the whole show was bivouacked in two massive apartment houses at the outskirts of Seattle. We were in a residential area and some miles from the show.

"Seattle World's Fair 1962."

The fair provided transportation to and from, but we were usually too occupied with the fair's events to utilize these perks. What a world of entertainment was to be found at the world's fair. When we had a matinee and showered off, we would pause only long enough to agree on which show we would attend next. There was a plethora of entertainment offered for our enjoyment or critical judgment, and with our entertainers' pass, we took them all in. Thinking back of the almost endless stream of top performers, now mostly dead, their names live on.

Liberace dressed in some dazzling costume and after an hour of nonstop playing said, "Excuse me while I go back stage and put on something a little more outrageous." Nat

"King" Cole with that mellow voice. I still have stacks of his old 78rpm records, and the memories they bring are rivaled only by the wondrous Ella Fitzgerald. We were there. We saw them all live. Johnny Mathias, Count Basie, the list seems endless; and each week brought in another star.

"Liberace and his dazzling smile."

A star of a different magnitude arrived but for only one show. Since our circus was working in the outdoor arena, we were given the day off in order that Billy Graham could take over the entire stadium. This was a revival meeting of gigantic proportions. The entire arena was filled, packed in by the thousands. We had never had a house to equal this, and they were not to be disappointed. After an impassioned sermon, threatening both fire and brimstone, he sent out his angels (yes, he actually called them "angels") up into the packed seats. They were a hundred strong and wielded two hundred buckets to collect the gratitude of ten thousand saved souls. I stood open mouthed, filled with disbelief and envy, as they trundled back into our commandeered dressing rooms, laden with the symbol of their purchase of salvation, just a one-night stand, no rigging to erect and only an hour's theatrical preaching. I heard the take was $50,000, and that was fifty years ago. Showbiz comes in many forms.

Still, the parade of fame marched relentlessly on. This particular momentous happening took place in what we call our backyard. We were lounging in the sun and wondering about the luxury busses parked at the far end. It was Elvis Presley come for a day's shooting for another emotion-filled drama titled, cleverly enough, *It Happened at the World's Fair*. We watched as "The King" sauntered out of his dressing trailer, clothed in an ill-fitting sweat suit, and called for his fiddlers four to come play catch with him. They tossed a football to and fro and seemed, from a distance, quite normal fun-loving guys. Then he lobbed a wobbly pass in Mary's direction; and she cradled it on the fly, kicked it back over his head, and turned away. "Whoa, sweetheart," he said. "You can join my team anytime." I was livid, but Mary simply said, "Bugger off!" And she went back into the building. I was king for a day.

It was autumn now, and the fair was drawing to an end. So too was our contract. It was time to talk about a renewal. I recall that meeting vividly. We had gone to some plush lounge to discuss a new arrangement. We had some snacks and a few drinks, and I remember the jukebox was playing, "I Can't Stop Loving You" by Ray Charles. It was a heady atmosphere and ripe for negotiation. The show wanted us badly, and we wanted badly to stay. I opened, saying we would need a larger salary, and they countered saying there was some German government restriction on the ceiling price for any one act. So they came up with a clever loophole. I would be appointed publicity and advertising director.

This would entitle the act to the same salary plus 5 percent of the circus gross income after all expenses were deducted. There, on the drink-covered table, scratched out on a paper napkin was what we might expect. Show's gross for a month: $100,000 less tax, expenses, salaries, etc.

LEE STATH (MARILEES)

leaving, say, $30,000 net. At 5 percent, it would give us an additional $1,500 on top of our monthly salary. We accepted, and I signed the new contract, but I had to confess that I knew nothing about the business side of running a circus. They assured me it was not a problem. It was only a title. I was merely a figurehead.

# Chapter XXXIV

# Mexico

THE PARTY WAS over, and the fair had come to an end. The show was moving on to another country. This time, it was Mexico. I knew Mexico pretty well. It was here I'd seen my first bullfight; and I was introduced, unceremoniously, to tequila. In a bar, just over the border in Matamoros, I recall a sobering sight. It was late afternoon, and only a few customers were nursing their drinks, waiting the evening's action. But the image that was stamped on my youthful memory was of an ornate bird cage hanging above the bartender's head. In it sat, side by side, a yellow canary and a Texas mocking bird. What a pathetic scene. The mocking bird was running through its full lengthy repertoire, including the canary's own unimaginative trills. The small yellow bird sat silent and drooping, on its tiny perch, imprisoned with this thief of song. I'm sure there was some philosophical lesson to be learned. But there were young girls and tequila, and I was one and twenty. No need to talk to me.

Back in Mexico, this time, the scene was much different being with the Berlin Circus, a new lucrative contract, and large beautiful cities to see. I see Tampico and am reminded of Stan Kenton's rendition of "Tampico." There was a grassy field through which we cut across, from our hotel, to get to the bull ring in which the show had been set up. As we brushed through the high weeds, dark clouds of mosquitoes swarmed up and engulfed our tender tasty flesh. That meant taking the long detour for the rest of the date. Then there was the beach at Vera Cruz where we trouped down with picnic baskets

"Circus Berlin's Goodwill tour in Mexico."

and swimsuits only to find the beach covered with small patches of solidified oil, a result of some distant oil spill or a passing tanker flushing out its bilges. Now Monterrey, there was a city to be long remembered. "It Happened in Monterrey." I wonder if that's why the song was written. Tony and I drank a bit in the nights after the show; and as we sat together, rehashing the previous shows, he suddenly blurted out, "I think I can do a 3 $\frac{1}{2}$." Yes, strong drink can do that, and I was in no condition to discourage him. So it was there, after weeks of practice and some encouragement but no success, I began to question the 3 $\frac{1}{2}$ as being a possibility. It was frustrating to both of us. There were so many little things that went wrong. Was it me? Was it Tony or was the trick really impossible? We brooded over it in the evenings. It was really becoming an obsession. After one of our morbid debates, Mary took me aside and asked if I was afraid of the trick. I was outraged. Me, afraid? I had hung for anyone and any trick. After she had calmed me down, she said, "I'm merely suggesting that you shouldn't lay back in the hole so long. I'd like to see you reach in and help him finish the trick. Don't expect him to do everything." I really didn't like that kind of criticism. It only aggravated me. Tony wanted to try it during the afternoon show. It was a poor house, so "why not?" The trick was high, a bit far, but I charged in, just for the hell of it, and I had him around the buttocks. We carried the trick past center before he ripped out and landed neatly in the front apron. Saints be praised, it was possible. We could do it. It was several days later, but there was new optimism; and sure enough, we caught the first ever 3 $\frac{1}{2}$ somersault during an afternoon performance. No one in the audience knew what we had accomplished. Yet it was circus history, and we were the first to have caught that impossible trick, and it put our names in the *Guinness Book of Records*. Still in disbelief and to convince ourselves, we repeated it that following week in Durango. Tony had become legend. Mary whispered to me, "Good show, Lee."

"3 $\frac{1}{2}$ saltmortal. Tony Steele to Lee Stath."

Life couldn't get any better. But as time would reveal, it could get a lot worse. There were, as all acts experience, periods of failure or more like slumps. We were having problems with the triple: some little hitch, the timing, the distance, the height. There are so many variables that must be perfect to catch a big trick consistently. That's the reason I was always so testy over the inevitable question, "Do you always use a net?" Certainly, we have seen the double trapeze and cradle acts working without a net, but few

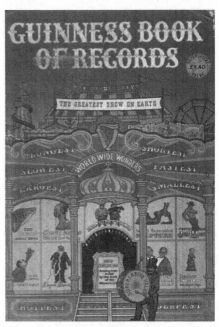

"Guinness Book Of Records."

people seem able to grasp the difference between a stationary catcher and that of a flying trapeze. Timing is critical. Laws of physics state that a pendulum swings at a fixed rate. A catcher in his trapeze is a pendulum. If the flyer is a millisecond too early or too late, leaving the pedestal board, there are going to be misses and replacing a flyer every week or so would be expensive and would give an act a bad name. Ergo: The Falling Wallendas. (Sorry. That should read The Flying Wallendas). It's true, there are a few catchers, who, sensing the error in timing, can shorten or lengthen their pendulum swing by contorting their body. But I grow pedantic. Just let me add, in all modesty, that Tony paid me the ultimate compliment when he told others, "Lee defies you to take bad timing that he can't compensate for."

Tony and I were buddies. How could a few misses spoil such a great act and forfeit such a great contract? Some speculated there was resentment or jealousy over Mary's tricks and success. But she wasn't about to limit her ability to placate anyone.

We opened the Christmas season in Mexico City in one of their largest arenas. It was a bonanza date where houses were expected to be overflowing every performance. Regarding my impressive title of publicity and press executive, all I did was wear a suit and tie, attend the newspaper conferences, and nod solemnly at what I deemed sage comments. My Spanish was not that advanced so I nodded a lot, but no one noticed.

The show was doing boffo business. Then, after a week or so, the director knocked on my door, one early morning, and said," Tony is gone.

"Lee, the press executive, preps Chimaro before take off."

His room is empty." It was a knell unto my ears. It was a shock to the entire show and not just to us personally. It was my responsibility to honor the contract to the show at least for this important date. We never missed a performance. Again, fate intervened. I was beginning to call it "Lee luck." Just across town (admittedly it was a very large town), the Atayde Christmas show was under canvas; and our old friends, the Flying Ibarras, were engaged. I had caught Nacho and Vincente (the two principal flyers in their act) before. So if one could dash over after their act and jump in with Mary and I, we might still have an act. It was only a matter of timing. (Isn't that what trapeze is all about?) Nacho or Vincente would phone and tell me what color costume they were wearing for their performance, then grab a taxi for the race across Mexico City, while Mary would try and match up whatever color they were wearing. One of the perks of this pandemonium was that there was no need to warm up for the show. They were warmed up and worn out. Bless those two guys. They alternated each other; but even so, on the big days, between the two circuses, they were doing five and six shows a day. At the end of the engagement, I spoke to our director and suggested that in light of our misfortune, they should consider taking the Ibarras in our place. With this agreement, Mary and I were, once again, left at the altar.

# Chapter XXXV

# Willy, I Knew You Well

IN THOSE DAYS, long ago, we were so resilient. We picked up our rigging, shipped it to the border at Reynosa then leisurely drove across Mexico to Acapulco. We found a secluded hotel, high on a bluff, overlooking the bay and moved into the fifth floor of the Hotel Sans Souci. Still together, we were indeed "without care." The balcony was ceramic tiled and served as both kitchen and dining nook. Sitting out in the balmy Mexican winter, sipping early morning coffee, watching the idle movements of boats in the bay, we had only to question what to do on the beach that afternoon. One could become addicted to Coco Locos, a fine and novel way of serving rum, if one were not cautious. We were cautious and after two weeks in paradise finally pulled ourselves together, loaded up the car, and headed for the border. We were back in familiar territory and also a familiar situation. With no place of our own, we headed up to Missouri where we had left our truck on Willy's farm, set up our rigging, and started practicing.

I feel Mary's brother, Willy, was character enough to be lionized in a book of his own. This letter I salvaged from Mary's discards. It was written to Mary by Bill's wife, Norine and gives a glimpse of life on the road back in the '50s.

Dear Mary,

Your letter rec'd yesterday. I shouldn't even answer it the way I feel. Guess I felt optimistic the last time I wrote, the joints must have got the nut that week.

We have had the damdest luck this year I ever heard of. When we first left San Antone we had to stay 24 hours in Waco getting new rear end in that truck we bought in San Antone. Paul did some amateur work on the old red junker and the next time he started it up the fan bit a big chunk out of the radiator and I don't know what else he did but from then on the clunker was in the garage every week and $17 was the cheapest it ever got out, fuel pump, valves, valve springs, carburetor. I didn't know there were so many parts to a truck. It wouldn't pull, it heated up and last week Bill gave up and junked it. Oh yes he'd put in all new brake system in it. He drove day and night last week, had to make four trips back with our tractor to tow stuff in. Got the trailers all in and set up Monday still had to get the trucks in. Put a new transmission n the panel the week before. New valves in our truck. The sea turtle died and we got a caiman. The goofs blew out both speakers and $\frac{3}{4}$ of the guts of the P.A. sets.

Tiger tried to drive the concession truck through our back door and it didn't fit. I've lost count on how many radiators that made for that clunker this year. It knocked Bill's rigging through the step and out in the kitchen but the rigging was o.k. thank God.

Bill put the truck we got in San Antone in the garage in Birmingham. $400, motor and transmission and it still doesn't run right. Had it in the garage here yesterday, fuel pump and I don't know what more.

Barney died in the middle of the night last week, and he wasn't even sick before then. So Bill is storing the shows and I'm glad. Those goofies were driving him nuts. Never a minutes rest. I don't think any of them could go to the donniker without asking him where it was and how to get there.

Whitey went to sleep coming in here (a 65 mile jump)!!! Rolled the panel over. The junk yard gave Bill $20 for it. Whitey was in the hospital 48 hours, they couldn't find anything wrong with him.

Write soon and come see us if you ever get the chance. We are all well (physically).

Love Norine."

An intimate insight into someone else's trials and tribulations. Bill, or Willy as Mary knew her younger brother, was a real rounder. His idea of a good time was getting drunk and fighting anyone in the bar. He was a circus actor from youth with extraordinary strength crammed into an average size body.

He was Mary's favorite. He was a menace to anyone including himself. In Norine's letter, his business had grown from wire walker, trapeze performer, and ultimately a high sway pole act.

He had a single pole, sectioned together in twelve-foot sections, stretching vertically, 120 feet in the rarified air.

LEE STATH (MARILEES)

This was held erect by stations of aircraft cable reaching out in a 150-foot radius. This was not store bought tubing but imported from Sweden. A pole of this length, swaying at thirty-five degrees, placed enormous stress on the steel. As a dare devil, not taking any unnecessary risks, he had each section Xrayed yearly, searching for any fault, weakness or defect. At that height, in a handstand, swaying to the extreme was a show stopper. So Bill added a second pole, situated 50 feet away and invented a changeover. In this, two artists would sway their poles in ever increasing arcs until they touched, grasped each other, and exchanged poles. In contrasting costumes, the effect was stunning.

*Bill Atterbury's* **SKY KINGS**

"At 120 feet, there was no room for error.
Bill Atterbury's Sky Kings."

Bill's enterprise was growing and required a number of riggings, trucks, trailers, and personnel. Bill had his own show and all the grief that comes with it. I'm not sure about the sea turtle dying but I guess he carried a side show as well.

Aside from the aforementioned tribulations, his real downfall began when he tried to top himself. Changing poles was innovative and gave him unlimited bookings. So he bought a helicopter with the sensational idea of having his performer carried aloft and deposited atop the pole. This was surely the ultimate in sway pole acts. To assure the fairs and parks of its safety, he would take the mayors and dignitaries aloft, and even with the engines silenced, the craft would flutter gently to earth. Bill was a showman, a businessman, and now a millionaire.

Too involved with the business side, he had taken on a partner, Darrell Hornbeck, a reckless athlete who relished the adrenalin rush of the sway pole.

"Bill Atterbury's growing empire."

They had a wonderful partnership. The act was a stunning success. An early matinee was scheduled, and after a great ballyhoo, Darrell was lifted aloft sitting underneath the helicopter. Things went smoothly as he was deposited on the sway pole's tip 120 feet above the grandstand. Maybe a downdraft or pilot error, but as the helicopter veered away, one of the skids tangled in the guy wires. With his own problem, the pilot revved the copter blades to the max trying to escape. The cables snapped, and he was free. The pole jerked, swayed, and another cable parted. Then one by one, like dominoes, they gave up. The rigging leaned left and then accelerated on its last thrilling show-stopping plunge.

Darrell wasn't killed. The 120-foot fall was only enough to cripple him for life. Bill was hurt nearly as bad only his injuries were not physical. Despite all his precautions and security measures, here was a tragic accident. He felt responsible for his partner's paralyzing plunge. No expense was too great to care for him, but this lone incident began to bleed his wealth away, that and his growing dependence

LEE STATH (MARILEES)

on drink. He let his show fall apart, would start new enterprises, and would lose interest when they prospered. His fifty acres of prime real estate in Springfield, Missouri, where he kept all his equipment, eight apartments for his working men, and an adjacent motel, all were lost. Earlier I questioned him why he had chosen such an innocuous place as Missouri to settle. His answer was simple and the reasoning sound. "Because I can jump to any place in America, in any direction and I'm halfway there. Any big contract comes up, those kinkers in Florida are still loading up, and I'm already there."

The winter we stayed at his place to practice, we sauntered out to our rigging and found him pounding stakes to double-anchor his rigging. I can hear him now, "God almighty, you finally made it. When the sun rose this morning, I was already up and walked two miles in the wrong direction." He was not beyond self-deprecation.

So he lost all of that. With his drinking getting worse, he finally lost his wife; his anchor. We were in Europe at this time and heard he had moved to Vegas. He loved the place. Nobody sleeps here, he observed. Then one drunken night, he was run over on the highway. We had come back to Vegas to work and saw his broken body pinned together in the local hospital. Pitiful sight but his spirit was just as strong as his body once was. Years later, we heard of him in the Vegas bars, leaning on one crutch and still provoking fights with strangers. He was finally taken in by his nephews in Los Angeles where he died of emphysema. John told of watching him lie there, breathing oxygen, yet bringing two fingers up to his lips and enjoying one last drag on his imaginary cigarette.

Remembering Bill's sad, sad finale, I find it petty to pick up my complaints as we settled onto his farm and began practicing with Ronnie Abbot.

Ronnie was the son of a former catcher who worked for Roy and Mary before my time. Ronnie was a mediocre flyer, a magician at overhauling automobiles and enough theatrical contacts that, between the two of us, we booked a profitable summer season for 1963.

LEE STATH (MARILEES)

# Chapter XXXVI

# A Fowl Contract

WE HAD JUST finished a date in Huntsville, Alabama; and the director of the prestigious Swiss National Circus, Herr Rolf Knie, came to visit and perhaps book us for a future season's employment. We knew and had worked for him in the past, an aristocrat of five generations of a circus dynasty. Formerly, he had tried to educate me in the European culture: dining etiquette; proper use of knife and fork; not only the judgment of a good wine, the nose, the palate, color and even the proper way to pour; never backhanded. How gauche. In addition, always cover the label with one's hand when serving. What a gourmet and connoisseur. So there we were at the local steak house in Alabama, trying to please and impress this sensitive palate with steak and potatoes. But perhaps a good, very good, wine would mask any of the deficiencies. I took the initiative. "The wine list, please." Our surly waiter glowered and replied, "We don't got no wine allowed in any eating joint. You want hooch, bring it yerself in a paper bag, and we don't say nothing. You want coke with it?" Such was the response from the maitre d' hotel. I excused myself, slipping out to the local liquor store, and returned with a paper bag full of "red hooch." Our guest was so amused at this American maladroitness that he agreed to our terms for a contract with his circus in 1969.

From Huntsville, we had a big, big contract in St. John's, Newfoundland. Much more money than we were worth, or so I thought, before we undertook the jump. I was certain I had done the math properly: two thousand miles in a two-ton truck in five days was reasonable. My error was the two thousand miles to St. John, New Brunswick, not the three thousand miles to St. John's, Newfoundland. All right, keep on the freeways; drive night and day; eat en route; pee in a coffee can; and, God willing, we'd make it by showtime. Things went as planned. We never turned off the engine for four days until we lurched into New Brunswick. Life and roads deteriorated. The truck was tired. We were no longer a circus act.

We had become angry enemies. St. Johns no longer seemed a destination but took on a veil like some unattainable holy grail. Then we turned off the weary engine. We had run out of road. We had reached Sydney, and I wondered if it could be Sydney, Australia. But no, this was now Nova Scotia, and we had some Atlantic Ocean to cross just to reach Newfoundland at Port aux Basques. So we parked on the quay and waited our turn to board the ferry. Time was passing and so were the other vehicles. We were being ignored. As the ferry neared capacity, I grew more panicky and went to the loading officer. I pleaded my case to no avail until a 20-dollar bill passed between us. We were quickly on board and on our way for the final and most grueling part of the journey.

All too soon, the crossing of Cabot Strait was done, and we were back on shore to resume the never-ending journey.

Six hundred miles to go and twenty-four hours left in which to make it. We could do it. The roads, though winding, were negotiable, at least for the first fifty miles. But as we left the coast and entered the interior, the road quickly deteriorated. Even in our state of exhaustion and desperation, we had to smile at the ludicrous road signs signaling a fifty-mile-per-hour speed limit. With four gears and a two-speed axle, we were relegated to second gear and a buttocks beating twenty to twenty-five miles per hour. Traffic was no problem, but it was threatening and frightening bashing our old truck through the ruts and rocks, passing through vast bare fields, and seeing rusting remains of vehicles pushed off the road and left to decay, unable to further proceed or obtain parts or repairs. Any increase in our

"End of the road."

snaillike pace would not hasten our arrival but only quicken the collapse of the old creaking, gyrating, stiff-suspension, heavily loaded truck. So the miles, barren terrain, and rusting relics jerked endlessly by. Nightfall came late in this high latitude, and the thought of arriving late for the show was unacceptable. We had never missed a show nor had been late. Time was running out, but the road wasn't. Halfway across the island, we were rewarded with a gas station, a full tank, all tires were holding, six candy bars, and the stupefying information that there were still 250 miles to go. Only twelve hours left. Maybe the roads got better.

We pressed on; and only the incessant banging, creaking, and groaning of the truck kept us awake and alert enough not to join the wasteland of earlier failures. I felt like a pioneer of old, crossing the vast prairies of the west. There was no difference

Even our arrival, at what I had come to believe was the mythical city of St. Johns, failed to arouse excitement or even relief. We had arrived, but emotion had dribbled out on the long trail behind us; and, no, this wasn't a city. It was a cold barren town, a fishing village at the most. Why would these dour citizens come to see a circus? Why would anyone promote a circus here on the outer edge of the continent?

We found the stock show building, backed up the truck, and unloaded. Four hours before showtime and there was the rigging still to be erected. We managed this in a trance like state and limped into the dressing room. It was full of all the other performers who were already dressed and bright eyed. God, how did they manage? They flew. All the other acts had flown in, gotten hotel rooms, eaten hot meals, and toured the town. That was the curse of a rigging act, always burdened with the heavy chore and then to climb up, trying to look fresh, vibrant, and entertaining. How we envied the "suitcase" acts. Those talented, gifted artists who needed only a few props to entertain a whole audience. Paul Seidel had a tiny Chihuahua he carried in his coat pocket. He made as much money as we; but, admittedly, his was a great act. We were booked for ten days, and our weary truck was parked just outside the back door. Some seasons earlier, I had transformed it from a hollow shell into a palace. Once the rigging and trunks were off loaded, we had an efficient kerosene, heating stove, butane for cooking, and a small

LEE STATH (MARILEES)

refrigerator. One small bed was ample for Mary and I. But this twelve-foot-by-eight-foot box was never intended to hold such crowds that descended upon us between shows.

"A box built for two but home to many."

I did not realize so many of these artists called us friends. I did not realize a lot of them could even call us by name. But there they were, huddled around our warm stove, leaning on the bed, lounging in chairs, and drinking endless rounds of coffee as Mary kept bringing fresh baked cakes and pies out of her oven. Yes, it was a long walk back into town where their hotels were, and there were now hints of snow and sleet mixed with a harsh wind that came in unabated from the North Atlantic. Still, it was pleasant being with fellow artists, talking "circus talk," hearing about others, their achievements and fates. I almost forgot about the beastly marathon that got us here and I didn't dare think of the return.

Now to the funny part. It was indeed a three-ring circus. There were, of course, no animals. After all, who would dare impose a journey like that on any poor animal? But wait, I tell a lie. There were animals, animals by the hundreds. This was more than just a circus. It was their annual livestock and farm show combined. The huge building was jammed with tables filled with an array of countless vegetables, mammoth things that were in perpetual danger of being eaten by the great herds of sheep, goats, pigs, and cattle. Then there were the poultry pens. What an extensive variety of feathery creatures. I remember asking the master of ceremonies when our act worked. He checked his itinerary and then said, "You're on, right after the turkey judging." Now we had followed a lot of weird acts, but this was a first. Unfazed, we waited our turn, climbed the rigging, and began our act. After each trick, the audience responded with enthusiastic applause. This was good; but something I had never before encountered was that a turkey, when startled, gobbles raucously, and when you put together a flock or herd or bevy of turkeys, you have pandemonium. When Mary would complete her trick and return to the platform, she would flaunt the response to Ronnie, our other flyer, saying, "I got a bigger gobble than you got." For a long time, we had our own personal joke: "I got a bigger gobble than you got."

# Chapter XXXVII

# Joe to the Rescue

THE PATH BACK from St. John's was the same but without the stress. We stopped at South Bend, Indiana, for a one-day date at the Notre Dame football field. They were emphatic that no holes were to be made on that sacred ground, but we pounded in our stakes in the dark. We shared the bill with Red Skelton, a really BIG fellow. The season moved on without incident, and we stopped off at Bill's farm to refurbish our equipment and always practice. Where were you when it happened? I remember well that November morning when we heard the shocking news of Kennedy's assassination. It really shook Bill and Mary, but the show went on.

Our last date was in Memphis, and we were staying at my sister's place. Ronnie was helping me pull the cover to reseat the valves on my fatigued Chevy truck when he casually said that he had changed his mind about going over to Europe with us. Bless him, he didn't run off in the night. He stayed and helped me finish the valve job and then was on his way. The Flying Marilees were on their way too, back to Sarasota with the monotonous chore of looking for a leaper.

With the rigging up, there was no shortage of friends who all wanted to stretch out and enjoy the pleasures of casual practice. But I was serious. Who could I get to leave family and friends and face the challenges of a foreign land? Joe Guzman? He was an old friend and half-ass flyer who showed some interest.

Being the off season, the trailer park was full of "recovering" artists. Everyone joined in the daily practices, but it soon became obvious that I was spending more time with Joe. It was no secret that we needed a flyer, but Joe? Friends took me aside at various times and cautioned me that Joe was nothing but trouble. How many acts had he worked with and what were the tricks he had accomplished? True, they were limited, but I sensed an untapped resource. My heart reached out and said, "Come, Joe, let me teach you to fly."

When the time came to catch the ship out of New York, Joe had developed into an acceptable asset to any flying act. As we set off for Europe, many shook their heads and admitted they didn't believe Joe could have blossomed into such a good flyer. From the beginning, I knew he had the potential if only given the chance and the belief.

We arrived, two weeks early, in Blackpool. Ample time for practice and let Joe understand the difference between an American, three ring circus and this intimate stage. They let us have the ring twice a day for practice and things looked rosy again. Even Mary grudgingly admitted the act would be OK. Then during a late-afternoon practice, I took Joe in a trick I knew was a little late in timing, but I knew I could hold it. Sadly, Joe's shoulder couldn't. He was finished. The doctor said with a year's rest and good rehab, he might be able to work again.

LEE STATH (MARILEES)

# Chapter XXXVIII

# Fool Me Once . . .

LESS THAN TWO weeks before opening! Jesus, Joe, pull yourself together. Allright, I was asking too much, but what to do? Joe was situated all right with his AGVA insurance, taking care of all his needs, but what to do? Word filtered through that Roger—the same kid that we had taken from San Antonio some ten years earlier, taught to fly, introduced into show business, and then had failed to show up in Copenhagen in 1960—was sitting dormant in London. I drove down, with my hat in my hand, and made him an offer he couldn't refuse and I could barely afford. Nevertheless, we opened on schedule; and the act was, once again, of the caliber of which we were famed.

We closed the summer season in Blackpool; and Knie, the Swiss National Circus, wanted us in Torino, Italy, for the winter date. Mary and I were still keen on the idea of camping out, and despite midwinter, we set up our tiny tent and with one sleeping bag to hold us we trembled the night through. Next frosty morning, the kindly camp owner insisted we stay in one of their small cabins and she would charge us no more. Each morning, when we entered the circus building, blue from the night's thrill of "camping out," Roger would greet us, boasting of his warm hotel room, the hot shower, and his first cup of steaming coffee. Whose act was this anyway? Yet I feel the Knie brothers, who booked a first-rate show into this massive arena, suffered far more. Night after night, we would go up with only a handful of spectators sprinkled, randomly, throughout the hundreds of available but empty seats. Even so, during our act, I could tell there was an audience out there; I could hear breathing.

Undeterred, they moved the show on up to Vienna, Austria, and a much more appreciative audience. This was an annual event, and for four weeks, we played before full houses. The end of the engagement culminated in a TV gala in which a host of international celebrities participated. These stars, in their own realm, tried to participate in some manner with the circus acts. France Nuyen, of "South Pacific" fame, fitted in nicely with the ballerina spectacle. England's premier football player made his appearance; but it was Gert Frobe, that villain of *Goldfinger* fame, that amused the masses playing a pantomime goalie. Interestingly, while with him, he admitted that he could not speak English. Then how, I asked, did he account for his dialogue in the Bond film? "Strictly phonetically. I memorized and spoke each line as it was spoken to me by my coach."

"Gert Frobe of *Goldfinger* fame meets the Marilees."

I didn't expect any celebrity to join us in the flying act so I was surprised when approached by the Wienerstadtsoper, the famed opera house in the center of Vienna, with the request that their premier ballet dancer would like to try. As one might expect, he was in superb physical condition: lithe, muscular, and handsome. But in addition to these attributes, he proved to be a most pleasant gentleman. A respected master in his profession, he listened and followed my instructions with avid obedience. After only a half-dozen practices he was able to step off and swing to me. As our arcs met, I could grasp his clownish costume by the legs and slip off his trousers. Stripped to his outlandish underpants, he swung back and forth, kicking and thrashing and finally dropping into the net, then running off stage. Being the beloved and renowned star of Vienna—Willy Dirtle stole the show.

"Will Dirtle; The lead dancer of the Vienna State Ballet."

There was great response in the local papers, and to show his appreciation for our efforts, he invited and seated Mary and I in the choice box seats at the prestigious Wienerstadts Opernhaus. A bottle of Dom Pérignon sat in an ice bucket by our seats, and we were his honored guests while he performed the male lead in the Swan Lake ballet.

# Chapter XXXIX

# Spain Beckons

IT WAS THERE in Vienna when Bucor, our agent, took us out to dinner in some small café; and we had the most glorious Hungarian bean soup. Over wine and soup, he laid out the contract for a season in Spain. There was the usual haggle over money, but I knew they wanted us badly. Mary's ability and blonde hair was an attraction that gave us great negotiating leverage. Still I was reluctant. The money was good and the promise of a long season was tempting. But I had heard from other artists, that in Spain, they often did three shows a day; and for an aerialist, that kind of physical abuse on the body, the tearing of one's hands coupled with the mental fatigue, could dull the necessary sharpness and quickly take away the pleasure of a good payday. Our agent, bless his larcenous black soul, consoled me with the words, "Artists! You know how they love to exaggerate and badmouth a show after they leave. And be sure they would love to see you turn down the contract and leave it open for them." This was certainly believable, but I still persevered. "Three shows a day, our hands couldn't hold out," I said. "Lee, listen to me," Bucor countered. "I've always been honest with you. Sign the contract. You've already got more from them than what they were prepared to pay. It's a good long season, and you'll love Spain. And I'll level with you. They might ask you to do a third show for one of the fiestas. Now am I being honest with you, or not?" It was late at night in Vienna. We had finished our dinner. Our third bottle of wine was nearly empty. I mulled over the idea of a third show, perhaps on Easter or Christmas. It wouldn't kill us. We drank to it, shook hands, and the deed was done.

The journey from Austria to Spain was uneventful. Crossing the border from France was a little different. This was the time when the great caudillo, Francisco Franco, was alive and ruling. Passing customs should have been simple. All our papers were in order, but the guardia civil—those proud, fierce soldiers who wore those shiny three-cornered hats that, legend says, were formed when they were forced, fighting, with their backs against the wall and their hats flattened but

"A protector of the people."

their spirit was not-these same protectorates of the people were suspicious of all the metal tubing that comprised our rigging and which we stowed under the truck floor. Could it be more than just steel tubing? Mary won them over with some photos of the act. "Ah, trapecistas!" Almost home free until one alert guard opened our bag of resin, that yellow hardened pine sap that we used on our hands and wrists to better grip and avoid slipping. It looked suspicious to them, and they took sides against each other whether it was uncut diamonds or a crude narcotic. I leafed frantically through my phrase book. "Where is the best restaurant?" and the other useful queries about my aunt's pen and the rest rooms. This might have gone on until Mary mispronounced "resin," and they all chorused, "Resina! But of course, for the violin." "Yes," I agreed, "for my violin." "Passe', amigos." And we began the tortuous trek through Spain. Not the nightmare of St. John's, Newfoundland, as this was the main highway into Spain. But still, prior to the invasion of Iberia by the hordes of Europe that would transform this idyllic peasant-populated paradise into a massive Las Vegas, the highways were still primitive. As were the people who would call you back and say, "No, señor, I said twenty pesetas, but you gave me twenty-five." Or "Excuse me, madam, did you drop your purse?" This is what we encountered throughout our time in Spain. Our journey came to an end when we reached the magical city of Seville. I am certain I will refer to other Spanish cities and villages as magical. But they nearly all were magical. I was reminded of the mortuary in Texas that boasted—"In business to serve you and your loved ones for thirty-five years." But to find a night's rest, in a Spanish parador, so elegant and regal, which had stood and served for two hundred years, now that was something of which to boast. It was magical.

LEE STATH (MARILEES)

# Chapter XL

# Sevilla, Spain

"Plaza Espana."

S EVILLE, SPAIN. WHAT a beautiful, ancient city. It
was their annual fiesta and rivaled Mardi Gras in
New Orleans or Carnival in Rio. In the vast area, reserved
for this event, we saw bare fields transformed into a small
town. Instead of mobile stands or tents, sturdy brick, rock,
and tile were used to erect theaters, dance pavilions,
cantinas, casitas, and stables for the all-important Arab
stallions that pranced and executed complex gaits at the

command of their proud Spanish masters while mounted on the rear sat the most beautiful, haughty, black-haired young women, dressed in the traditional flamenco, tight-waisted, flared, colorful costumes of an enviable past era. As they strode through the crowds, they were met, time and again, by appreciative patrons offering them small dainty glasses of their famous dry sherry or Jerez. They accepted these expected gifts with perhaps a nod, but the dignity that their dress and manner exuded kept them aloof from the commoners on foot.

"Fiesta on foot was for the commoners."

All this theater and drama amid the backdrop of the beautifully assembled structures that could stand for years but were all torn down, with no evidence of their existence at the end of the two-week celebration. But what a two weeks it was. The circus alone was only a small part of the offerings, but can one imagine the conglomeration of five, count them, five, competing circuses? Each one was a massive, four-or six-pole, canvas-covered behemoth. This was the big date, and no expense was spared to bring in the best acts, entertainment, and a brief respite from the daily drudgery of the workplace. Although it was hard to imagine a job that gave its workers a full three-hour break for a bodegas offerings and a siesta being hard work. Within these bars lay a virtual cornucopia of cured hams. These hogs roamed free in the hills, grazing on lush grasses, pungent herbs such as wild rosemary, fennel, thyme, and acorns that, combined, did so much to flavor their meat. This was the jamon serrano derived from the black Iberian pig from the Grenada, Huelva, and Lerida districts. Each very strictly authorized and guaranteed with the producers' metal stamp of authenticity. After being cured in the cold, mountain regions for seven months minimum and sometimes years, they now hung like bloated bags from the ceiling with small plastic cones attached to the bottoms to catch the oozing oil as it seeped through and out of the aging meat.

"Serrano hams aging in an ancient bodega."

Then there was the tapa bar. To take a stool; order a vino tinto or a glass of Jerez; and then run the gauntlet, visually, of the gastronomic display. What to order? I had once made the error on my first visit to Spain and being famished for a Tex-Mex meal of seeing "tortilla" on the menu, I ordered half a dozen. My waiter was gracious enough to persuade me to try one, and if I liked it, he would bring me more. The large potato, onion and egg omelet overflowed the plate, and one was more than ample. So I added the word "tortilla" to my Spanish vocabulary. But here at the tapa bar, now a seasoned gourmet, I was frustrated over the display of various olives. Olives stuffed with cloves of garlic; olives stuffed with anchovies; olives stuffed with almonds; and then green, black, and purple olives immersed in oil, brine and a piquant pepper-laden liquid. And this was only the olive section.

Moving right along, with a dry sherry in hand,

"Lee tests the wine's bouquet."

I hesitated, momentarily, over an assortment of tiny, whole, deep-fried fishies. "Some of those, por favor." Oh, and the squid! How many ways can one prepare them? Whichever, most of them were on display. My plate runneth over, but the bar continued. The aforementioned ham lay in paper, thin slices, sausages of many varieties, chorizo, my favorite, and small, thumb-sized green peppers that were panfried upon your order in, guess what? Olive oil! To sit at the bar or choose a small table under the stalactites of ripening ham, watching the Spanish businessmen or day laborers, conversing and consuming these plates of tapas, at five or six in the evening and knowing that by ten they would be sitting down, with family, for a full proper meal. Why weren't they fat? For that matter, why weren't there any drunks? We've frequented the restaurants and have seen the families, large gatherings with children, which were sometimes boisterous and vocal, but wine was a part of the meal, shared by all and abused by none. Perhaps that was the secret, not a forbidden fruit. So with the workday behind them (interspersed with a two-hour siesta), the Sevillianos were eager for a little diversion; and here at these vast fair grounds, everything, for the family, was offered. I can only speak knowledgeably of the circus, but I have never stood on a midway and seen five different circus fronts all grouped together.

# Chapter XLI

# Angel Cristo

THE SHOW, ON which we were contracted, was called "Circo Aleman" or the "German Circus." No one is a hero in their own town, and so it was the norm to pass off one's show as not only the biggest and best but also of foreign origin. What more could the public ask? Still, it seemed odd that five of the biggest and best circuses in the world were all grouped together and each coming from some foreign land just for this spectacular event. Interestingly, the owner of our show was a Greek but had come to Spain many years previously, married a shrewd Spanish gypsy, and had a handsome son named Angel.

"Angel Cristo; son of a Greek and a gypsy wench."

Our Greek director had transformed the normal four-pole tent into a six-pole megaplex. Take that! You other four-pole rag bags. And to fill it, he had brought in our own capable flying trapeze act plus, at the other end, flying in the opposite direction, the "Flying Jarz."

So here was our first introduction to a Spanish fiesta and not two weeks of three shows a day, as I feared, but five shows a day. When I charged into the director's office, cursing as best I could in my Mexican Spanish, he tried to mollify me, not by producing my signed copy of our contract where I had, indeed, agreed to three shows a day during fiestas. Instead, he praised our extraordinary performances and stated how pleased he was to have us on his show. He understood our complaints. But this was their big engagement, a chance to reap great rewards that might be needed to see the circus through tough and leaner times to come during the long season. And after all, he had agreed to our unprecedented financial demands. Still, he sympathized with our dilemma. Consequently, he suggested we cut out one performance and let the Jarz work alone and then give the Jarz a break one show, when we would work alone. "But that's still four shows a day," I protested. "I understand," he assured me, "but your act is so strong. We have put out so much publicity about you . . . still, I am a reasonable man and understand the physical demands of an act of your kind, so cut out one trick in your last performance. It will be missed, but I am a reasonable man."

So I left the office, pleased that he was so satisfied with the act and getting to rest for one show and cut out part of another. Wow! Deep inside, though, I had the feeling I had been diddled.

We had long competed with the Jarz throughout Europe. Armando's big trick was a two-and-a-half pirouette return to the trapeze from the catcher's hands, a very impressive and tricky trick. We had agreed to pause until its completion; and they, in turn, waited until Mary's big trick was done.

It was amicable enough for two acts working together but reluctant to concede any advantage to the other. We managed to keep it that way for the two-week engagement, though Armando and I were never really close friends.

Two weeks of the Seville Fiesta, despite the grueling schedule, went by swiftly. There was so much to see, so much to do, and as a performing part of the fiesta, we were welcomed to all events and the endless activity.

I had no idea I could dance flamenco until I was pulled on the floor by a beautiful raven-haired, gypsy wench with the most colorful frilled dress, cinching her slim waist and flaring out yards of lace and sequins around her black high-heeled, shoes. Oh, how sensuously she moved. The ensemble of guitars and clapping of hands, her twisting, haughty, teasing, tempting dance forced me to reply, forced me to join this physical flirtation. Somewhere, deep inside, unknown to my consciousness, I was part gypsy. I was flamenco! Or was I a fool? The party was hysterical with laughter. Mary had averted her head and refused to acknowledge knowing me. Only when the young dancer pushed me mockingly back to my table and the Spanish men enveloped me in their uncontrollable hilarity, slapping me on the back enthusiastically, embracing me with rough, good-meaning hugs, congratulating me for my bravado, bringing endless glasses of wine, yet advising me to stay with my circus job and never try dancing again. Not any kind of dancing. Only then did I fully realize I was not a gypsy. I was not flamenco.

Closing night came, and we tore down our riggings. I was on the canvas top, slacking off our mainfalls, always careful to walk, or more accurately, creep along the tent's lacing. I would never conquer my fear of heights. Though I could not see the circus ring, I knew it was bare and lying sixty feet below. I watched Jarz's muscular catcher striding fearlessly across the canvas, cutting the distance in half that I carefully treaded. I had to admit he was a better rigger than I. They would be down, packed, and out before I could let my boys below get our rigging on the sawdust.

I didn't see it, but I heard him shout, not a scream, but a definite shout at the same moment the canvas opened. The ripping sound of heavy rotten canvas all but drowned out his cry as he slipped through the long, jagged tear in the tent. I dropped down and clutched the heavy laced section. I was fearful that the whole tent was going. But nothing moved. Light spurted up through the jagged opening, and I could see my agile opponent, lying twisted on the ring fence below. He was making terrible sounds. He was moving. He looked alive.

Well the engagement was over. The hospital was efficient, and the Jarz had a new catcher in two weeks. They missed a few beats, but the act was nearly up to its norm in a month or so. The act, a truly Italian family act, never thought a moment before bringing their old catcher along, though his fall had cost him his right leg. They found a place for him on the show, and this was long before there were any benefits or disability compensations for circus artists. He was fortunate to be among those who cared.

Armando Jarz died a few years later in Lisbon when he ripped off the fly bar on his return from his feature trick, that two-and-a-half pirouette. He bounced out of the net and broke his neck on the floor below.

The party was over. Flashing lights, streets thick with soggy confetti, all were quickly extinguished or washed away. Concrete and rock walls that took weeks to erect were gone by midday. Our rigging was loaded, trailers hooked up to trucks, and we were ready to move on. But to where? All the other circuses, with whom we worked, issued a route list at the beginning of the season, naming each town and date where we were to perform. Not so in Spain. All day we sat on the deserted fairgrounds. Only the gypsy camp at the far end, with their tents and corrals of magnificent horses, remained. I queried the tent master repeatedly. He assured me "In due time, tranquilo." How could I remain calm with our future so uncertain? Yet the other artists seemed unconcerned and went about their normal activities; some went shopping, dinners were being prepared, a halfhearted soccer game developed in the dusty field. I approached the German act, Concha e Concha, and asked if they knew anything. Siegfried said he wasn't sure, but he had heard some talk of Malaga. "Great!" I said. "But why all the secrecy?" "Well, you've seen for yourself, there is much competition here in Spain. These five circuses are only the tip of the iceberg. The country is full of family shows, dog and pony shows, rag bag circuses, all eager to get into town a day before the bigger shows open." He was distracted, momentarily, by an errant soccer ball that he footed deftly onto his head, balanced it a moment, and then kicked it well over the heads of the complaining players. "When Senor Cristo gets all the information and data he can collect, he'll decide at the last moment. Then we go." This was maddening. "How can you put on a show with no advance, no publicity?" I asked him. His trailer door opened and Dieter, his brother, eased out, stripped to the waist. "Mensch, it's hot today. You ready to go, Lee?" "Well, yes, but your brother doesn't know any more than I do. How can a show operate like this?" Siegfried explained my concern for showing in a town with no advance billing. "Oh, that doesn't matter on the small dates. If we fill half a house, that pays the nut, and that's all Cristo is concerned with." The soccer ball intruded into our conversation again. Concha e Concha scuffled in the dirt until one kicked it back into play. "Wait until we see some of the big dates. There will be paper all over the town, weeks before we get there." Siegfried nodded. "You'll love Pamplona. Eight days there, and you'll be lucky not to fall asleep during your own act." "You mean another fiesta? Does that mean five shows a day?" I asked hesitantly. "Herr Marilees, that is what circus in Spain is all about." Grinned Dieter. "We follow the fiestas."

# Chapter XLII

# A Marriage Multiplies

THE SEASON GROUND on and the whole of Spain was celebrating some saint or virgin, sometimes both at the same time and staggering their festive, religious patronage throughout the complete year. I found myself thankful when we would break up a long jump between the big cities and stop for a one-or two-day stand in some wayside village. That would warrant only two shows in the cool of the evening. What a respite. But that meant driving all night over unpaved, patched paths of tar and gravel, with the constant threat of wandering cattle and arriving at dawn, with time enough for two espressos and a bag of churros before the physical challenge of setting up the rigging. Then a cold shower with a bucket of purloined water. By now, Mary would be back with her bicycle ladened with fresh food for the day. Sometimes she pedaled five kilometers. Other days she was blessed with shorter excursions to the marketplace. But always on her return, as she went about her small well-equipped kitchen, preparing what the locals had proffered, be it snails, squid, frog legs, or pheasant, she would be filled with this excitement that exuded glowingly from her; the little church she had found with some extraordinary sculpture or the paintings, fully exposed yet obviously priceless. On lucky mornings, she would catch the mighty, antique organ during its practice, and when the boys' choir was in rehearsal, her morning was complete. All this, plus the picturesque town folk she encountered, was painted vividly to me as she effortlessly produced and lay before me, fresh, clean, healthy meals that made my hours of physical labor a well-rewarded joy. Small wonder we flourished both physically and spiritually, day and night, always together.

"Shampoo in the rain was an unexpected luxury."

Our love was forged in that strenuous, sweaty, physical atmosphere. In those close quarters, we couldn't turn or stand without some contact. It was sweet, and there were only two shows that night and we could move on and do it all over again the next day but in a different surrounding. But now it was July, and we were heading for Pamplona and San Fermin.

# Chapter XLIII

# A Bunch Of Bull . . . .

**R**EADING HEMINGWAY AND Michener can never prepare one for the actual experience of Pamplona in July. We arrived several days prior to the opening, which gave us time to settle and prepare for what we were assured would be the most unique eight days of endurance one would ever hope to see. We were early enough to explore the city before the invasion of the outside world.

Riding our cycles over the aged cobble streets; sitting outside at the cafes; watching as they erected the wooden barriers that would corral the stampeding bulls and steers down the narrow streets, ahead, behind, and over the panic stricken, drunken, half-crazed throngs that seized these few moments of real danger, to come out unscathed, or bruised, perhaps bleeding but hopefully alive and suddenly very much alive. More so then they had been for years back in Sweden or Germany or

"A tribute to Hemingway in the Pamplona square."

America. Here, they had come close to the real challenge and survived. Not all of them. The daily papers carried the list of injuries, minor and severe. The greatest danger was falling among your comrades and being crushed under the pile of onrushing hoards, all trying to get over the top. This was all yet to unfold, but for the moment, we had the privilege of being the few early outsiders. Sipping the bitter espresso and watching the feverish preparation, I was struck by the atmosphere of something big to happen, an electric field of current that ran through the city and all its people. It happened every year, but it was as if it were new and they were every bit as anxious and excited as would be the thousands that would soon invade this staunch fort.

July 7 came. The bulls and steers had been corralled, near the center of the city, at the top of the street. Before I touch on the carnage that followed, look at it from my privileged point of view. The first circus performance was not scheduled until ten that evening. There was far too much action, during the day, with which to compete. First show was full. Second show, at midnight, was packed. Things began to flow together. Was it the third show now or the last? We came down from our act, not bothering to undress, only pull down our tights, loosen our supporters, and wait for the next show. Five times we went out. Five times we climbed up the rigging and wondered if the shouting, cheering crowds might be the same people we had just entertained two hours previously. One outstanding feature that couldn't go unnoticed was here at four thirty in the morning, front row, were hundreds of enthusiastic people; but sitting in their midst, jumping up and down, clapping, laughing, and shouting, were little children, toddlers: four-, five-, and six-year-olds having the time of their lives. This was July and San Fermin, and I suddenly felt rejuvenated. Always high, after a good performance, there was no way we could sleep.

In a matter of moments, we were out of our wardrobe, makeup removed, and on our way with the surging throngs to watch the running of the bulls.

Two glasses of wine for breakfast. This was madness, and we had not been inoculated against it. The bulls ran, people got trampled, it was over in a blur of minutes. Still, we

"I hope they don't run too close. This is my best suit."

danced and drank and followed the rush to the bull ring. The choice was ours, to join the demented daredevils in the ring or watch the mayhem from the stands. We had had enough "daring of the devil" with five shows so we opted for a safe seat and cheered the foolish lads who crammed the arena. As the gates opened, out charged a young steer with its horns capped in leather pads. But this did nothing to cap his enthusiasm as he charged, full bore, into the huddled masses. Bodies flew, a few flashed improvised capes in what was meant to facsimilate the matador's moves but invariably resulted in the loss of a good towel or blanket and more often a twisting, laid-out somersault. The steer seemed inexhaustible, turning on a dime or someone's buttocks. He was everywhere seeking satisfaction. The only recourse the challengers had was to flail the animal with a rolled-up

LEE STATH (MARILEES)

newspaper. One inebriated lad, he had to be American, thought the best tactic was to try his ability at steer wrestling. This did not go well with the more knowledgeable challengers; and they turned on him with a vengeance, pummeling him to the ground with fists and feet. After all, it was explained, a steer deserves respect and there are rules. He had not read the small print. More steers were let in; and it was touching when a man was butted, tossed, or trampled into unconsciousness how the nearest group would lift his prone body, high over their heads, and carry him over to the ring fence and hand him to waiting arms where they received immediate, very professional care. The hospitals were well staffed and prepared for these inevitable, daily occurrences. But enough of this hilarity. The sun was up, and we were becoming aware of a growing weariness and began the slow, trek home. Still, we were not the only ones feeling the need for rest. As we walked through the streets and cut through the parks, we had to pick our way carefully over the prostrate forms of men and women, boys and girls, that had curled up or fallen down and lay immobile. It reminded me of a scene from Nevil Schute's *On the Beach*, where a nuclear war has laid the entire populace, peacefully on the ground.

Once in bed, exhausted from twenty-four hours of rushing adrenaline, I found it hard to sleep. The thought of being inside those barriers,

"*On the beach* in the Pamplona streets."

waiting for the rocket to explode, watching for the first wave of runners and then the tight huddle of black bulls pushing them down the street and toward me. After all, I was an athlete and I could do this. To be in Pamplona in July, to be at San Fermin in July, one had to run with the bulls. I lay on my back with our one electric fan humming, and with my decision made, sleep came easily.

It was almost noon when we awoke. The heat was oppressive in our small tin-roofed truck. I wanted to sleep more, needed to sleep more, but the sweat was seeping onto the sheets; and already we could feel the throbbing of drums in the distance and the wailing of pipes and horns, shouts of revelry meant this was not the time for sleeping but the time for fun and frolic. We dressed quickly, deciding to forego breakfast and join the crowds at our new popular cafe. Too early to drink, what with our five shows to consider, plus, I had decided to take my chances with the bulls next morning and wanted nothing to dull my instincts and reflexes. Still, as we dined on the Spanish tortilla, some gambas, and three thimbles of black espresso, we found entertainment enough, watching the drunken orgy that spiraled around the square. Wine truly flowed as freely as water, and everyone danced with everyone. I have never seen such a drunken, rowdy throng, pushing, shoving, dancing, and singing; but not one incident of violence did I see. Certainly, there was the omnipresent Guardia Civil that would be quick and efficient at subduing any action they considered improper. Anyway, there would be violence enough tomorrow morning when they, no, we, would test our machismo with the bulls. Mary must have suspected but said nothing when I purchased a pair of white pants and a red

LEE STATH (MARILEES)

kerchief to go with my white T-shirt. We moved among the masses, enjoying the religious relics being carried on the burly broad shoulders of the many participating devotees of the many competing churches, each with their own saint or virgin, each vying to outdo the other, all with ornate splendor bedecking the massive, ponderous floats. The men struggled valiantly, their thick hair and faces lathered in sweat. Then on some silent, given signal, they stopped and slowly lowered their precious burden. Here, the cafe, bar, and shop owners would proffer them with botas and glasses of wine. A moment's rest; their thirst temporarily slacked and their strength renewed, they resumed their purpose, picked up their passion, and fell in behind the marching band and slipped slowly through the narrow streets and, without touching a wall, executed a sharp, right-angle turn around a corner.

Now weaving among the masses was a horrifying Gigante. His huge grotesque head swayed to and fro, while under his cape and gown, he stalked his prey on wooden stilts. This lurching demon was three meters or, as we say, "ten feet tall" while in his hand he waved a gnarly club made of foam rubber. This he used to thump the small children who danced and squealed with delight, knowing this mock punishment absolved them of past sins but with no guarantee of future misgivings. To my surprise and unsuppressed glee, Mary (though she was sinless) caught the full wrath of the Gigante; and he flailed her blonde head a half dozen times before she escaped, screaming like a girl, into the safety of the crowd. We could have stayed there all day, mingling with the polyglot of all the nations, but after another stupendous Spanish meal of grilled lamb chops and a simple salad, we knew we must rest if we hoped to get through the evenings ordeal of work and still make tomorrow's bull run.

Once again, more through rote rather than showmanship, we struggled through the night and all five performances. The tent was still full for every show. Once again, we slipped out of our tights, washed off our makeup, and I put on my white outfit with the red bandana around my waist. I might not be flamenco, but I knew I had a good chance

"Ten feet tall and still growing. San Fermin's saints."

of running with the bulls and not getting hurt. "I hope you know what you're doing," Mary said as we left. "Catchers are not easy to find in this crowd." With this encouragement, we set out for the morning's activities. Filled with confidence, I leapt with agility over the barrier and joined the raucous, early-morning dare devils and sacrifices to the bulls of Spain and the worshipers of San Fermin. I was about to become a believer. I heard and saw the first rocket explode in the early misty dawn. The bulls were loose! There were hundreds of fervent fools between me and the bulls. I had chosen, or had been advised, to keep away from the outside corners. All I had to do was keep plenty of people between me and the cows and stay away from the corners. The shouts and cries from the street above told us that the Mongols were coming. All of civilization was doomed. Only I stood between that threat. At the far end of the street, I saw, or rather

I felt, the surge of flailing bodies being herded and pushed forward by the unified nucleus of bovine bullies. I stood my ground. If panic overtook reason, I could still vault over the wooden wall. Though I now saw it was crowded with cheering, taunting spectators. *Come down here and fight like a man*, I thought, but then the bulls were upon us. I was mesmerized as I watched the unity of power rushing headlong toward my sanctuary.

People ran over people. Bulls and steers ran over people; and I would, unhesitatingly, have run over people, except there was no place to run. Just as suddenly, they were gone. It was over, and I had "ran with the bulls in Pamplona." Well, I had not exactly ran. I had stood, transfixed, as the bulls ran past me. But why quibble over semantics? There were more pertinent issues at hand. On the sharp corner of the street, which I had been advised to avoid, a massive, muscular, black bull had slipped on the cobblestone road. When he went down, he snapped the bone in his left hind leg. He was up in a moment, but the thundering herd was gone; and, disoriented, he turned to face his tormentors. I was not one of them. The sight of this powerful creature, charging at anything that moved and with that dangling broken appendage made a gruesome sight. While the remaining men folk tossed and waved pieces of clothing, the monster wheeled left and right, unable to fully use his strength and anger. This encouraged the "wannabe" bull fighters who moved closer and thrashed their makeshift capes against the froth-covered head of "El Toro." I was closer than I liked, and when a young German lashed out at the bull, his elbow caught me in the throat. "Shit," I grunted and swung hard at his bare head. He went down quickly with a "verdammt" oath, and I heard the crowd behind the barriers roar. Unsure whether it was approval or disapproval; thumbs-up or thumbs-down, I dove under the wall and escaped through the crowd.

I got home before Mary, showered, and made a decent appearance when she returned. I was relieved when she fixed our supper with no comments. But later, just before show-time, the director called me upfront to the office and said he had heard of my antics. It was the only time he appeared truly angry at me. "I didn't hire your act to come here and play around. You work for me. You don't take chances, and if you get hurt doing anything outside your act, I'll cut your pay." This was not our first experience with this authoritarian leadership. In Switzerland, the contract forbade any type of skiing. Sunburn was forbidden in England (fat chance); and a vague clause, in Italy, colorfully phrased, was meant to restrict over consumption of alcohol. One of the most unique clauses, found in our contracts, was that Mary was not allowed to cut her long blonde hair during the engagement. I didn't mind that. I liked her long blonde hair and I didn't know the first thing about skiing. But as for the bulls, well, I didn't intend to do that again, ever.

"Mary the Medusa."

LEE STATH (MARILEES)

# Chapter XLIV

# Swinging On A Farm

A NOTHER OPENING, ANOTHER show. We had secured a year's contract with the Chipperfield's Circus, an English show that was moving to fresher fields, a long way to go for fresh fields. We were to open in Cape Town, South Africa, for the Christmas of 1965 and stay for the season of 1966.

In our artistic environment, we have had the pleasure and good fortune to meet many celebrities and famous persons. Yet one incident comes to mind of a simple farming couple that stands vivid in my memory. I had so much tonnage of extra rigging, a baggage trailer, and what seemed like endless trunks of personal junk; I was desperate for a place to safely leave it for the coming year. Roberto, our agent, said he knew of a farm in Belgium with ample space. He contacted the owners, and we were welcomed. It sounded ideal. So we trundled our collections across the Channel and headed on down to the farm. It was perfect. All the space needed without imposing. We met the family, and they were most congenial: Herman, the owner, and Hilda his wife. I guess they were typical, hardworking Belgium farm owners, both stout, perhaps fat but outgoing and friendly. "Put your gear near the barn, and no one will bother," Herman assured me.

"But come. You will dine with us tonight." We were tired from the long drive, and a night's rest would rejuvenate us for the coming trek. Dinner was pleasant, though not exceptional, but these were simple farming people. Imagine our surprise when, after our meal, we were presented entertainment. We were ushered into the living room, given a glass of sherry, and introduced to their eight-year-old daughter. She came in with a vague sort of Spanish dress, ruffles and all. Thus began an hour of an uninterrupted presentation of a Belgium's idea of flamenco dancing. The young child was determined, though talentless. She tortured her captive audience with repetitive stomping, prancing gyrations accompanied with poorly manipulated castanets that clashed dangerously near our frozen smiles of appreciation. This was interspersed with frequent shouts from her proud parents of "Ole! Ole!" which, loosely translated from the Belgium language, means, "Sock it to 'em, sock it to 'em." I thought she would never stop. But in retrospect, I wish she hadn't. For when the child was taken away and put to bed, our hosts unveiled their true hospitality. Herman, the fat farmer, suggested we spend the night in their house and forego the primitive bedding in our old truck. A nice gesture until he made an overt offer that I should share his wife, while he and Mary could find other arrangements. The fat old farmers were a couple of swingers, an awkward situation. Somehow I declined the tempting offer without offending. We bid them adieu and left that night, driving like the wind for the English Channel, hoping that would put enough distance from that unsavory situation. That was over forty-seven years ago. We never went back. I wonder what Herman did with all that stuff I left on his farm?

LEE STATH (MARILEES)

## Chapter XLV

# Life On The Rails (Again)

OUR ARRIVAL IN Cape Town was well documented by both press and newsreel. We, on the other hand, were equally impressed by the vast changes of the Cape Province. The docks and waterfront had been transformed into an inviting social center. Expensive restaurants and boutiques now lined the previously dreary waterfront. Africa was changing minute by minute. Still, at this late date, there was still apartheid. There were separate performances, one for the whites and another for the blacks. During the latter shows, our costumes were carefully monitored, particularly Mary's. Accepting these forgotten mores, we were soon back on the road or, in this case, the rails.

Life during our seven-year absence and despite the development and progress had changed little for us aboard a circus train. Our living compartment was no bigger.

"You are sentenced to 52 weeks in this six by seven foot cell . . . but we called it *home.*"

The narrow gauge rails were no wider and the jumps no shorter. Africa, from a circus view, was unchanged. A one-day stand in a tiny dorp (village) named Ogies gave us a priceless addition to our growing resume. The following day, the circus revue in the "Ogies Blat" raved over the performance and stated, "Circus Chipperfield presented 'The Flying Marilees,' which was the greatest flying trapeze act ever seen in Ogies." The glowing editorial did not mention that it was the only flying act to ever appear in Ogies. Such was our growing fame.

Moving once again on an all-night jaunt, we had two steam engines in tandem to pull and jerk the long loaded circus train to the next indistinguishable town. Sleep was difficult as the coaches lurched and lunged throughout the night. Near dawn, we were stopped again, a long pause, back in reverse, forward again, and then the long sigh from the two tired engines. Back to sleep, hopefully. But that's when the oncoming freight rear ended our stationary section. God bless our tiny compact compartments. There was nowhere to go but snug up against the bulkheads. We were uninjured but incensed at this negligence. I picked myself up and bolted out of the coach. Daniel, the crocodile man, was beside me; and we raced down the track to the offending engine. We had no problem in pulling the engineer from the cab as he was too drunk to resist. Enraged as I was, I had to pull Daniel away as he pummeled and would surely have kicked the unconscious engineer to death. But enough damage had already been done. As the dawn broke, we found the rear most wagon, the elephant wagon, crushed, splintered, and derailed. On the tracks lay Rosie, an old elephant cow, dead. A blessing there were no other injuries but a big financial loss to the circus owners. Yet is there a loss with never some gain? As the brutal South African sun rose, the native boys were quick with their knives; and the Zulus took first choice at the throat and shared the warm blood with themselves. Fresh blood from such a mammoth beast assured them of even greater strength. But in a short time, Rosie was distributed equally among the lesser tribes, an amazing moment of sharing. Soon the wreckers and crane arrived while we were left to assess our personal loses. I then became aware of my feet, bare from my bedroom dash and now embedded with thick broken thorns. I limped, painfully, back to our coach and lay on our tousled bed; while Mary worked diligently, probing and digging the stubs of thorns from my now swollen feet. Still, a small discomfort compared with what might have been and the loss of sweet tasty Rosie.

After the excitement was over and we were back into the routine of two a day, we still had time to relax and observe life in the nineteenth century. The train arrived early, but the tent was slow going up. Someone had pushed the layout man off the train during the night. So we had time to go into town for a store bought breakfast. Mary and I entered the café, already filled with the locals. We had become adjusted to the awkward silences and covert glances. But in this tiny town, when we took our table and sat in what felt like near nakedness, the patrons dropped their newspapers, sat with half-raised coffee cups, and opened mouths; while those with less advantageous views simply turned their chairs 180 degrees and faced us with unabashed awe or bewilderment. This must be what the aliens of the future might expect. We ordered two sticky buns and coffee, to go and we went.

Of course, not all of South Africa was so antiquated. I remember a sunny, free afternoon in Johannesburg. We joined the gang and went to the local swimming pool. It was an expansive layout with two separate pools of crystal water, one shallow and one deep. The manicured lawns were lush and green with deck chairs and lounges scattered throughout. We frolicked, dove and swam, and finally took refuge in the warm sun and soft grass. We snuggled up close, embracing the beauty of nature and the joy of being together. That's when the life guard came down from his tower and very politely pointed out that this section was for men, and the ladies were allotted an equally lovely part on the other side. Men and women were not allowed to lie side by side in the same area, no hanky-panky in the park.

Suddenly, another year was gone, and we did our last show on New Year's Eve. We were, once again, in Johannesburg; and it was midsummer. We rode with the show down to Cape Town where they prepared for their new program and its 1967 opening. We, on the other hand, prepared for the leisurely two-week journey up the West Coast of Africa. We had almost boarded the Royal Mail Ship, SS *Durban*, when that same unshaven lad of eight years earlier appeared with a large bouquet and wishes for a bon voyage.

It was Keith Anderson; and he had somehow gotten to England, picked up our old net, and started his own flying trapeze school. Good luck to him.

LEE STATH (MARILEES)

# Chapter XLVI

# Genuine German Beer

DORNIGHEIM WAS THE winter quarters for the Franz Althoff Circus. We drove silently in, parked, and headed into town for a taste of genuine German food and beer. Herr Althoff proved himself to be a gentleman and admirable circus director. Our act was in good shape, and we looked forward to a profitable and pleasant season. The show opened in Austria. The public's response was so good that after the three weeks in Vienna, we closed and moved the show ten kilometers to the other side of that fabulous and historical city. We set up for another three weeks and had equal success. There were over a dozen "straw houses." A straw house is that enviable situation when all seats are sold out and the people are still clamoring for tickets and admission. Ring boys are sent to the horse tent, and bales of hay are broken open to be spread around the hippodrome track, and the overflow crowd is seated on the straw. Working before that kind of enthusiastic audience is inspirational, and the word "work" is a misnomer. What a blessing to find a profession that is more rewarding than the money received. It was after one of those exhilarating shows that Mary and I joined Bubi, the elephant trainer, for a late-night dinner. Bubi was a true elephant man, massive in size and character. He boasted that the elephants would call him at night if there was any discomfort or friction among the herd. I do know that just before the show, he would group the performing elephants around him and command them, "Piss! Komm, Gerta, Piss" And those that should, did. He always brought his herd into the ring, clean.

Bubi knew Austria and spoke glowingly of a gasthaus on a lake only twenty kilometers out of the city. That was another fascinating element of the big, European cities. A short drive or a hearty bike ride and you were in the green forests, lush fields, brooks that actually babbled, and a serenity that has existed here for centuries, excluding the years of brutal warfare. But this evening, all was beautiful and still. We circled around the isolated lake, black in the night except for a glittering reflection of the old Gasthaus, nestled at the head of the placid water. We parked, and as we approached the entrance, we could hear the ump-pah-pah throb of a small German band. Through the door and we were absorbed into this pulsing, joyous gaiety. Beer was flowing, dancing was energetic, but the aroma of solid, dependable German food was our welcome and evening's goal. We took our table and accepted, without question, three steins of dark beer. Ordering was simple. They offered us selchfleisch und kartoffel klosse. That was a tender sweetly smoked pork chop with a unique potato dumpling both lathered in a thick simmering sauce. There were more savory side dishes, we had worked hard, so we ate well.

It was nice being away from the circus atmosphere. No one knew us, and no one noticed us; we were part of a simple festive evening with amicable strangers. As we sat, watching the revelry of elderly couples, dancing to the familiar old German tunes, we were happy, infectiously so. Life was good; and we were young, filled with good food and more beer to drink when our attention was drawn to a sobering sight. The front door opened

"Gluttony in a German Gasthaus."

slowly, and two old haus fraus eased through. Held between them was an ancient bent gentleman with sparse white hair. Even at his age, which is always difficult for a young person to measure (he must have been ninety), he possessed the traditional white handlebar mustache. Though pure white, it was impressive in its thickness and size. We watched, Bubi, Mary, and I, with mixed emotions as the two old women eased the gentleman into his chair behind their table. We turned our attention back to our own table and beer and fell into deep, philosophical discussions of life, death, and the undignified curse of old age. What things had this old derelict once achieved? What joys had he once experienced? What passions had he once felt in earlier days? It was poignant, and we could have continued the discussion far into the night had we not been interrupted, suddenly, by the old man himself. He stood, now erect, at our table, made a courtly bow, took Mary's hand, and said, "Kom wir tanzen." With that, Mary was on the dance floor, and indeed they were dancing. Not just one polka, but then a Foxtrot, and finally a slow sinuous waltz. It might have further continued had Mary not begged off, complaining of a sore foot. He returned her to us, clicked his heels nobly, and left an exhausted young girl and two stunned young escorts.

LEE STATH (MARILEES)

# Chapter XLVII

# The Enigmatic
# Herr Nickstadt

HERR FRANZ ALTHOFF called me into his office to meet an unusual man with an unusual request. He introduced me to Herr Gerd Nickstadt, a film director and producer of some note in Bavaria. I shook hands with this tall distinguished longish-haired gentleman who appeared to come from some noble ancestry. His accent was the Hanover Deutsch or the elite "hoch Deutsch." But after the pleasantries were exchanged, I found he spoke English with an Oxford nuance, but in deference to Herr Althoff, he expressed his wishes in German. He had a young boy, an actor, whom he wished to film as a trapeze performer. Would I consider teaching him the basics in order that he might be passed off as a circus artist in his film? Herr Althoff agreed, we could use his circus and lights after the last show, and I could train the boy. The monetary offer was staggering, and I readily accepted. After Nickstadt left, Franz took me aside and said he wasn't sure he liked the idea. He was certain that the film director was homosexual. I hadn't sensed that, but the proposition still looked good regardless of his religion. So entered Frank Rheinboldt.

A boy of seventeen years, typical German, blond hair, high cheekbones, exceptional physique; in short, a handsome lad. His English was basic, but he appeared eager to learn. I believe one of my strong suites is in teaching. So I undertook long nights in the still circus arena, just Frank and I on the rigging while Nickstadt and Mary watched. The show, ever mobile, moved on; and

"Frank, Mary and Gerd Nickstadt learn the film business."

with it, Frank would follow, crisscrossing Germany, practicing late and always the presence of the film director himself. We became good and close friends; and true enough, he was, as suspected, a homosexual but also a true gentleman. While working in Berlin, he had us stay at his home. He lived as one would expect a movie director to live. His apartment, in the heart of the city, consisted of four floors. The uppermost floor was fitted out solely for his young protégée: a massive room with tumbling mat, a side horse for vaulting, and a trapeze in the middle of the room with space enough for an actual full swing. That kept Frank happy. Even as impressive was the vast apartment studded with paintings on every wall. Each staircase had old seemingly priceless works of art at every stage of the landings. Broad windows looked out on the panoramic central square of Berlin. In the basement was a large sauna and an eight-meter heated swimming pool. We enjoyed his hospitality and generosity to the point where I said, "Enough of your paying me to teach. Your friendship is

LEE STATH (MARILEES)

enough." Nickstadt made his film, Frank was the star, and the whole thing was a bit of a fiasco.

Still, things went on as usual. Nickstadt and Frank cropped up, over the years, to appear in Spain, France, Italy, or wherever we might be performing. One late evening in Segovia, they arrived. Mary was frantic, trying to provide the usual exotic meal for unexpected guests. I had only one bottle of an insignificant red, which would not do for such a discriminating gentleman as Herr Nickstadt. So he and I motored into the outskirts and found a bodega as unpretentious as a bar in New Jersey. Still, after sampling several offerings, we both exclaimed, "Aha!" It was a Rioja, Marques de Riscal of a vintage year, which meant little to me at the time; but we gathered up six bottles and returned to our "truck home" where Mary had somehow scrounged, found, and prepared a real Spanish paella. Where she found squid, clams, mussels, and shrimp is still a mystery but not a surprise. Throughout our lives together, I have come to expect this from her.

# Chapter XLVIII

# The Ugly Duckling

LET ME TELL you more of Mary's kitchen and how it came to be. The renaissance of this undeniably ugly vehicle began in London in 1971 where we were rehearsing a Christmas TV show with Billy Smarts Circus for BBC. I was desperate to replace the terminally ill Chevy truck I had shipped over from the States years earlier and was keen on following a lead regarding a salvage yard across town.

We were set up in the tent with heaters and a first-class catering service when I saw Tommy Turnbull across the ring. He was juggling five broiled shrimp onto a plate full of assorted tidbits: smoked salmon, pate, small crackers with faux caviar, rare roast beef, and a large Guinness. "Tommy, you freeloading clown, what are you doing here in England?" He made no covert action as he slipped the entire contents into his baggy trousers, save for the Styrofoam cup of Guinness that he lifted, and said, "God bless you, Lee." Tommy had had a problem with drink for a long time, but he looked good. "I thought you were in South Africa still," I said. "Got a good contract with Jerry Cottle. Twenty weeks guaranteed: but, God, Lee, this bloody weather. I tried washing my truck when I got here, and the bloody water froze. How do they expect you to be funny or even clean in this kind of weather?" Poor Tommy, how long could he last away from sunny South Africa. And of course, the antipathy that had long existed between the English and the Afrikaners did nothing to assuage his self-brought misery. "Cheer up, Tommy. It's only one season." I hadn't the heart to tell him that the weather in England could make or break a fragile character. We shared a few more Guinness's, a couple of laughs, and he embraced me in a big bearlike abrazo and said, "I love you, man." A few more pocketed shrimp and he was gone. It was just a year later; and we were at the Christmas show, in Berlin, when our agent casually mentioned that Tommy had shot himself some months ago in Scotland in his stalled truck on the frozen roadside. You were funny, Tommy. Why did you lose your sense of humor in that dour Scottish countryside?

I followed the salvage yard lead I'd gotten from Francis Brunn, the incredible German juggler on our show. He was so incredible and talented that during the Big War, Adolph Hitler himself gave Francis free reign to perform throughout Germany with no threat of serving in the armed services. A great talent preserved. So with his instructions, I took the underground to Leicester Square, boarded the red double-decker bus, another transfer, and I was let off in Clapham Common. Here was where I found an old salvage yard, crammed with derelict war relics: half tracks, gun turrets, armored vehicles of various types, a wealth of fascinating remnants of the Great War. I could have spent days rummaging through this museum of rusting metal, but I had a more pressing mission. And there, in the back lot, stood a half-dozen identical Thames Trader trucks. They had been the pride of the British Air Force and were equipped to service the air force bases as a mobile grocery stores. I prowled through the rusting rows of hulking heaps. One promising prospect had been stripped of its radiator; another lacked integral engine parts, but they were all thirty feet long and had a hungry potential to be converted into a home. I pressed on in these wet cold typical London surroundings, stopping at another old retiree. It looked the same. The interior was wet, crammed with empty grocery racks on either wall. A massive dead deep freezer chest stood up front. The three large skylights were open, so maybe the roof didn't leak. My imagination raced ahead. I saw picture windows where now bare walls stood. I saw plush benches; a kitchen with unlimited cupboards; a kerosene heater radiating warmth and comfort; perhaps a shower with running hot water; and, somewhere, a bedroom suite. This old hulk could be a home for someone with the passion and ability to make it so. I jumped out, splashed up to the office, and found the greasy manager. "The old Trader there, the one in front, will it run?" "Don't know, guv, 'aven't tried." It was futile to conceal my eagerness. It had to run. It was going to be my home for many years, and it had to run for many miles and through many countries. "The keys! Give me the keys." I gasped hoarsely, grabbing at his filthy lapels. "Bloody, crazy Yank, it's got no battery, 'as it?" I swallowed hard. This was no way to bargain. So I tried the casual approach. "If it runs, I'll buy it." Now I had him in a corner. He fished out a ring of keys, stuck a few wrenches in his pocket, and led me out to the field of dreams. With some effort, he heaved a single massive six-volt battery out of a gloomy shed and trundled it over to my home. Once installed, he told me to give it a go. The battery was good.

LEE STATH (MARILEES)

It whirled the sleeping engine repeatedly, slapping it around the head and shoulders, demanding a wake-up call. My heart was pounding. I'd stopped breathing. "No go," said the man who held the mortgage to my future. "Bloody things been sitting too long, needs bleeding." "What?" I jumped out. "What are you saying? Bloody? Bleeding? I thought it was diesel." "Daft, Yank. Get your arse back in and crank it when I tell you." I climbed back into the cab. I was pleased to see he was warming to me. So with a lot of cranking and a lot of bleeding, I heard a cough and then a roar. I was ecstatic and terrified. This was a cab-over-engine, snub-nosed diesel, and the engine was naked, sitting beside me in the cab. Blue smoke surrounded us. It coughed, sputtered, and returned to a deafening roar. I shouted above the din, "it's alive!" "OK, mate. Come inside, and we'll settle up." Once again, I became the cool calculating American business type. As we entered his office, I asked," How much?" "Four hundred quid," he replied. "Done," I agreed.

In an hour, I was on the highway, creeping cautiously on the "wrong side" of the road; plus, the four-speed gear shift was in my left hand while the steering wheel was on the "wrong side" too. I pressed on with ever growing trepidation and a heavy heart. What would Mary say? With traffic streaking past this juggernaut, I forced myself to test my white elephant. With engine roaring, cab shaking, and my foot flat on the floor, I risked a quick glance at the speedometer: fifty miles per hour. It felt like a hundred. I eased off, swallowed hard, and ignored swift mobile autos flashing by. I took the proper exit (one of the few times in my life) and entered the terror of town traffic as I crept toward the sanctuary of the circus grounds. It was at these slower speeds, turning sharp corners and yielding to other traffic, that the impact of what strength was needed to negotiate a ten-ton truck with no power steering or power brakes. But I had made it from the junk yard to the circus lot without incident. Things were looking up. Switch off, hand brake on, and I eased out of the cab. "Good Lord, what is that?" Mary queried. "This is our new home." And so it was.

"Thames Trader Lorry. Not a pretty sight."

"Mary's kitchen in the Ugly Duckling."

"The house that Lee built."

LEE STATH (MARILEES)

## Chapter XLIX

# Nickstadt Shows His Hand

IT WAS A short while after another Pamplona marathon that we crossed the Rio Tajo and entered the fortress city of Toledo. The circus lot was a flat plateau of landfill made of gray, white clay. God help us if it rained. We would all be. mired there for eternity or the sun came out and baked the quicksand dry. But we had no rain; and the sun stayed out, blanching and reflecting off this arid, dry, dusty moonscape. Yet we could look over our manmade precipice, just above the Rio Tajo (Tagus), and across, only a cannon's shot away. There on a verdant steep hillside stood the reconstructed Alcazar. The hallowed bastion that withstood the siege in 1936 from the Republican armies, and though hopelessly outnumbered, the Conservatives withstood the onslaught for seventy days until the arrival of Franco's forces to liberate the few remaining survivors amid the rubble of the proud once-great fortress. Rebuilt, once again, for even Napoleon had his hand in laying to its destruction, having burned it to its foundations. Now it stands square and squat, impervious to invaders until, one can only guess and fear, its next invasion and destruction.

It was here, in this somber setting of Toledo, that Herr Nickstadt reappeared to visit. He had not brought his young protégée, Frank, along. Consequently, my evenings would not be spent trying to coach, coax, and coerce this young lad into serious practicing. Though Frank was capable, his short attention span contrasted with a plethora of talents that led him down many artistic paths yet all leading back to Nickstadt and the reality that success in any field required the dedication and hard work he was unwilling to give. Now here on our ochre dust-blown lot with the show set up and ready, we had the time and temperament to indulge ourselves with Nickstadt's unrestrained generosity. Where this noble, aristocratic gentleman earned his fortune, we were never certain. One painting on his staircase was, he admitted, a questionable but probable original oil of the Brahms family, if so, of great value to the Brahm's foundation and worth some millions in Deutsch Marks. He was waiting to have it authenticated and if proved to be "the" painting, he was undecided whether to sell or move it upstairs into his bedroom suite. Gerd Nickstadt was born into a wealthy family, educated in Hannover and London; and though his proclaimed profession was screen writer and director, it seemed as though he was always in the process of scripting the "great circus story." When he was not with us, extracting truths and lies of circus lore, he would be back in Germany or the south of France, being entertained by the wealthy dilettantes that so admired his work and art collection. But as we grew to know him and enjoy his company, his elegant manners, his eloquent storytelling, I suspected he was in demand as a person of stature and entertainment. He was meant to be the guest of the wealthy play people throughout all of Europe.

LEE STATH (MARILEES)

## Chapter L

# In Over My Head

THIS WAS BACK in the '60s; and the then famous and beautiful Brigitte Bardot had married Nickstadt's billionaire friend, Gunter Sachs, who was the heir and owner to the Opel Auto fortune. At times we were included in these overlong weekend soirees. Nickstadt had assured us that this particular one was a simple informal affair. Still, I chose a suit, white shirt, and tie; but then I had only one suit and one tie from which to choose. Nevertheless, it was a tailored, handmade, double-breasted, conservative cut I had made in Paris. I was all right. Ever anxious to make a good impression and knowing the company into which we would be thrown, I wanted Mary to dazzle these pseudosophisticates. As we dressed in the cramped confines of our truck, I clutched a beautiful blue-and-gold brocaded dress she had tailored in Bangkok, purely oriental with its high collar, skin-tight waist, and hugging her hips. With that sensuous long slit from hem to midthigh, we might just forget the party. "No," she said emphatically. "Not the right occasion." I clawed frantically at her extensive wardrobe, but she pulled a plain black dress out and said, "This will do. I'll wear the pearls you got me in Tokyo." *Oh, big deal*, I thought and I was reminded of the pendant diamond earrings I had bought for a birthday present some years earlier. She had been pleased, but then she looked quizzically at them and said, almost unbelievingly, "Why, they're for pierced ears." I readily agreed and told of the simplicity of having one's ears pierced. I recalled during the war, when we lost a crewman topside, during a crash dive, we younger sailors vowed to wear an earring in memory. The gunners mate on board said he could fix us up in a moment. Sitting me down, in the small galley, he held an ice cube on either side of my left ear for a few moments. Then with a cork to back him up, he forced a long sail needle through my lobe, cleansed it with alcohol, and inserted a broken toothpick through the puncture. "That should do until we finish the patrol, and then you can fit a proper ring. Take two APCs and call me in the morning." No wonder they had made him a gunner's mate. "OK, thanks, but what was the deal with the ice cubes?" I asked. "That was to numb the pain," he boasted. "Well, dammit, it didn't work." I didn't relate this sea story to Mary but insisted it was a simple procedure. She loved the earrings and said she would have them changed to the screw on or clip types, but she was adamant that she would never have her body disfigured by any outside invasion. How ironic was that statement that only the future would reveal.

So we joined the gala, me in my best suit and Mary, prancing proudly ahead, with her high heels clicking, her tight black dress moving and her long blonde hair swaying. Maybe she wouldn't look too badly next to the glittering movie stars: the jewel-bedecked tycoons' wives and the bevy of young beauties who were always invited to flesh out the crowd. What an overwhelming sight it was, as we were escorted into this vast, sumptuous heavily chandelier ballroom. It was, as I expected, more than I expected. A twelve-piece orchestra was sequestered in a far corner. Tuxedo-dressed waiters and more flamboyantly costumed servants moved silently among the guests. Though it was slated as an informal affair, one could detect the touch of several famed haute couture masters. Our host was gracious. Mary was quickly swept away. I was introduced to a magnificent lady, laden with jewels, a countess of some significance, as "the greatest flying trapeze artist of our time." "Of course, you are, my dear. Sounds terribly exciting." And she was gone. I was beginning to suffer and I watched Mary, wonderingly, as she moved confidently, not from group to group, but new groups seemed to form around her. Slowly she made her way around the hall, and finally, we were together for a moment. "Having fun?" she asked. "Well, the wine is pretty good, but what the hell do you find to talk about to these people?" was my query.

"Nothing, really. They seem quite content to talk about themselves. I just listen. Actually, they're fairly descent folks, for town people." And then she was rushed off to meet someone of "great stature." I could only stare and wonder at this petite figure as she was surrounded by a new configuration of males and females alike. How had she, in a plain black dress with pearls, won over an entire ballroom?

"Brigette Bardot, my escort for the evening."

I would try to mingle and pass light pleasantries. Though my German was good, I was under pressure trying to maintain a semblance of understanding in the small French-speaking groups. Brigitte, whose English was little better then my French, tried to put me at ease. But invariably, I laughed at the wrong times or nodded gravely at some hilarious joke. I did create some levity when I took the floor after some of the most expensive and driest champagne I had tasted was endlessly served. I stood the mocking crowd before and begged their indulgence. I related an experience of a few years earlier in the French-speaking part of Switzerland. We had just completed a big engagement in Lausanne and were driving along the beautiful Lake Leman to our next date in Montreux. It was past midnight when, unsure of directions, I stopped at a bustling inn. I entered the door and asked, in my best French, "Excuse me, but where is Montreux?" I was ill prepared for their reaction. Coffee was spilled, beer spurted out noses, cups crashed on the floor, and the entire cafe fell about laughing. The smiling innkeeper took me by the arm and out the front door. He pointed to the fork in the road and said, "A droit." Through all of this story, my captive audience listened politely, nodding knowingly, and chuckled appreciatively. They had seen the punch line coming early in my narrative. So be careful if you travel through Switzerland and wish to visit Montreux. Perfect your French pronunciation and don't ask some stranger, "Ou' est mon trou?"

After this bit of repartee, I moved about the massive lounge from group to group, stopping only long enough to hear what language in which they were conversing. This

LEE STATH (MARILEES)

was not always easy as they seemed to flow effortlessly; and it seemed, unknowingly, from French, Italian, German, and English. It depended on how emphatic or which tongue best conveyed their ideas and thoughts. I wandered about the throngs in this great hall; and though I had dressed well and my host and his guests all greeted me cordially, I felt ill at ease, definitely, out of place. I had the feeling that I had stepped in a pile of elephant dung and was smearing a spoor, carelessly, across this priceless Persian carpet. Mary, on the other hand, was across the room in the center of an animated group. I was eager to get back to the sanctuary of the circus.

# Chapter LI

# Nickstadt's War

WELL, THAT WAS then, and this was now. Put-up day in Toledo and Nickstadt was there for a visit. We could look forward to a most enjoyable week. He had taken lodging at the local parador, Virrey Toledo, and we were quick to promote a ride in his rental car and check out his choice in this historical city. The parador was once an ancient monastery and was now a luxurious inn. In which many of the expensive tapestries, rugs, and paintings still adorned the huge dining room, halls, and individual private rooms. Gerd (Herr Nickstadt) had chosen a suite with a balcony overlooking the city and a view of the River Tagus. "Exquisite scenery, money well spent," I stated. "Now can we use your shower?" asked the two sweaty Philistine guests. Hot water and an enclosed bath was a luxury sorely sought. After we were refreshed and more companionable, I mentioned that the dining room downstairs looked very inviting and asked him to be our guests. "No doubt, the parador has the finest quality, but I remember a place, not far from here, that serves some of the finest roast suckling pig in Spain. I will take you there," insisted Gerd. "We yield to your superior knowledge and delicate palate," I said while elbowing Mary to be silent. With no show tonight, I felt we deserved an evening of fine cuisine and great wine. It was always a certainty with Nickstadt. Though it was early evening and the Spanish don't begin eating before eight, we motored off on a small paved road that Gerd vowed was just as he remembered it, though it had been a few years since he last passed this way. We all knew things did not change quickly in Spain; and it was, as he predicted, only a short drive. Then there on the left, not more than ten or fifteen kilometers south of Toledo, set back off the road, was this huge parking area and this unpretentious restaurant secluded among a large growth of ancient oaks. There were tables outside, under some lights, where a few early guests were conversing and sipping wine with assorted bowls of almonds and olives. "Looks lovely," Mary ventured. "How long since you were last here?" "Not more than four years or so, but I never forget a good kitchen.

Come. If we're too early, we'll simply talk and drink good wine." and he ushered us inside.

I have no intention of trying to describe the interior or the magnificent meal of crisp roasted suckling

"A simple Spanish dinning experience."

pig and creamy mashed potatoes sprinkled over with blanched almonds. A simple Spanish salad and Gerd waved away the house wine, in favor of a vintage Rioja. They had an extensive wine cellar. No, I won't elaborate, except to say, it was a wonderful delight; and I have tried to relocate this restaurant several times but with no success. It was during this exceptional meal that I displayed, once again, my ingenuous personality. I am a notoriously slow eater and always believed it was the proper way to savor and enjoy a meal. Gerd, on the other hand, rushed through his plate with no hesitation and, I believed, no appreciation. "Gerd," I admonished, all knowingly, "you've got to eat more slowly, taste the delicacy of each bite, savor the exquisite efforts of the master chef." "Sorry," he replied, touching his lips lightly with a linen napkin." But I have a bit of a medical problem." "Oh," I countered, "like you're only allowed to enjoy a fine wine?" "Something like that. I'll tell you some other time." After a local liquor, and a cup of espresso, I persevered. "So why can't you enjoy a leisure meal? What's your hurry?" "Well, I had an injury, and if I don't gulp my food down, my throat constricts." He explained. "Sorry," I acknowledged. "What kind of accident?" Gerd did not seem the reckless or adventurous kind. What, I wondered, could he have done to warrant this disability. In our profession, I knew I could match him injury for injury. "Was it an auto accident?" I probed "Driving under the influence, I'll bet." "No, no," he replied. "Nothing so mundane as that. It was late fall." He paused; and I could see his mind looking back, searching for the words, the experience, the memory. "Very late fall in '42. That would be some twenty-seven years ago. We were in Russia, advancing, and as forward reconnaissance my partner, Gunther and myself, had just emerged from a forest with no sight of the Russians. Then as we struggled through a dense thicket, we almost stumbled into a stream of running water. There had been a fairly heavy snowfall, but the water was not yet frozen. We had been in our uniforms for three weeks and much longer since I had bathed. Seeing

LEE STATH (MARILEES)

the water still flowing and the thought of scraping off the filth and stench that had become part of all of us, I was tempted, momentarily, to strip down and rid myself of the disgusting accumulation of putrefaction that had slowly become a part of me. But before this thought could manifest itself, I became aware of my right index finger. I had, long ago, cut away the thick insulated glove that protected this, my trigger finger, from the Russian cold. How was one expected to fire the heavy weapons we carried with these clumsy mittens was a question not answered in the Wehrmacht manuals? I wonder how many German infantry soldiers, who survived that madness in Russia, are missing that digit; that trigger finger? But my chilled finger was still sensitive enough to warn the rest of my body to keep its filthy clothes on and not to get wet. My comrade and I moved a short distance along the riverbank to a small bridge. There were no tracks in the snow and, to this point, no sign of the enemy. In a burst of exuberance, Gunther shouted, "Last one across is an ass hole." I was in no mood to frolic, much less run. He was only a pace ahead of me, one foot on the bridge, when he did the most ridiculous thing. He leapt three meters up into the air, turned halfway around, opened his mouth wide, but said nothing. Then I realized why I couldn't hear him screaming. I didn't even hear the explosion. I couldn't hear at all. The buried land mine had catapulted him into that acrobatic execution, but the intensity of the blast had been directed back toward me. I dropped to my knees and suddenly felt most pleasantly warm. I could see my rifle was next to me, but the snow was quickly turning from white to red. I was distracted, momentarily, as I saw Gunther dancing and jumping in front of me. Had he gone mad? His silent ballet was most unnerving, and slowly his hoarse whispers grew to a full-volume scream. "You're going to die! You're going to die!" And yes, I guess I was. I wanted to tell him to shut up, but it sounded instead like I was gargling; and yes, I guess I was going to die. I couldn't breathe. Blood was draining down my throat. My neck was torn open. I ripped off both gloves and grappled at my gaping wound. Each gasping attempt to breathe sucked more blood into my lungs instead of the bitter cold air I was dying to find. I was not aware of my probing, grasping fingers thrust deep inside my throat. But I do remember the moment I sensed the tube my fingers found and slid out of my opened, bloody neck. What told my fingers it was my severed windpipe and what surgical knowledge told them to pull it out and suck in that desperately needed air? I had lost a lot of blood, but as long as I could keep my air pipe outside that gory mess, I could breathe and, even perhaps, live. Gunther finally collected himself, returned to our outfit for help, and the rest was a lot of hospitals, operations, long, slow rehabilitation, and now very little scaring. Thanks to an old, Jewish doctor. Ergo, my need to swill down my food, quickly as possible; but, still, with great enjoyment, which brings to mind a quote by the ancient Greek philosopher, Epictetus, "Preach not to others what they should eat, but eat as becomes you, and be silent."

We were all silent, finished our coffee, and went outside to find a pleasantly, cool evening and a quiet drive back to the lot. Gerd dropped us off at our truck. It was now late, and we said adieu for the night. Mary and I slipped quickly under the blankets, we hugged each other affectionately, and I kissed her as I felt her slip guiltlessly into sleep. I lay there, alert, wide eyed, and sleepless as the night of silence ticked slowly away. Gerd, my good friend and once a hated enemy. Some years earlier, I would have rejoiced in his death. Yet now, in our friendship, I too suffered in his suffering. Bloody war. Bloody propaganda. Bloody shit. I dozed off.

# Chapter LII

# It's Only Money
# And Sentiment

SHORTLY BEFORE DAWN, Mary elbowed me and suggested it was time for coffee and an early start for really seeing this historical city of Toledo. I slept on the outside of our minimattress so it had long been the custom for me to arise and brew the morning coffee. This was no simple prosaic procedure as I had developed a complex recipe of three imported coffee beans, all to be ground separately and blended into a carefully calculated formulae of rich espresso. It was strong, it was black, and it was bitter; but it started the day off with a bang. I didn't need that first cup to bang me awake this morning.

As I moved into our living room, com dining room, com play room, there on the floor, blocking my way into the kitchen, was Mary's purse, wide open. Its contents were strewn across the floor. I grunted, puzzled, since I had long grown used to Mary's paranoia of hiding her purse in a different place each night. This was not one of her hiding places. I stepped over the debris, reluctant to accept the obvious. I made the coffee and sat down among the treasured remains. Such a puzzling convoluted assortments of rejects. Her Japanese pearl necklace was gone; the diamond earrings; two thousand five hundred American dollars she always kept stashed away for that inevitable crisis she knew was only around the corner; they were all gone. But most heart-wrenching was the eight-diamond-encrusted wedding ring and last, the one-and-a-half-carat blue-white flawless diamond solitaire I had bought for her in Cape Town. That gouged me hard in the belly.

Back in South Africa in 1958, the owner of Boswell Wilkes Circus had introduced us to his friend, a diamond merchant. I well recall his asking us into his office wagon. That in itself was an honor and an introduction to South African circus luxury. Sitting on this narrow gauge track was one entire-length railway car of much extravagance. The interior walls were of a deep rich mahogany, illuminated softly with cut-glass chandeliers and plush zebra-skinned sofas. Black natives hung discreetly in the shadows, and he bade them serve us our desires. English tea is always good, but we were eager to see the African diamond rings. In good time and in a casual manner, the diamond merchant rolled out on the hard teakwood table a cloth of black velvet. This was a nice touch. I tried to casually sip my tea, but my inner self cried out, "Show me the ring!" He opened a small leather pouch and poured out a dozen stones. Quite a sight, but where were the rings? He sorted them in size and then asked what I liked. I was out of my league. I looked helplessly to Mr. Boswell, but he touched my sleeve and said, "Trust him. He is a master jeweler and a friend." "Well, the big one is my choice. I want the best for Mary," I said.

With what I would later describe as a condescending smile, he replied, "If you want the best, young man, look closely at what you call the BIG ONE. There are some minute carbon flaws I could point out, and, though a large stone, it has only half the value of this smaller one-and-a-half-carat blue-white gem. This is the stone we jewelers compare all other stones. This is a rare perfect diamond. If you want the best for your wife and can pay for it, this is the one." Mr. Boswell nodded. "He knows." The price, mounted in platinum, was 500 English pounds, almost $900. We took it and blessed those poor black natives digging somewhere in the mines nearby.

That was gone. I brought Mary her coffee; and we sat on the floor together, counting our losses. How had they, or he, come into our cramped truck, found her hidden purse, and then seemingly sat five feet away from our bedroom, took these priceless treasures, and left orderly placed on the table top our passports, driver's license, work permits, and less valuable junk jewelry aside. Of no value to them or were they so considerate as not to create the hardship of reestablishing ourselves in a foreign country?

LEE STATH (MARILEES)

# Chapter LIII

# A Leader Of Men

ON A LIGHTER note and still with the German Circus, we had a free day. Eager for some more hedonistic pleasures, we opted for the local cinema. There was an American film showing, and though not in English, we didn't hesitate to join the crowd. I don't recall the name of the movie, but we thoroughly enjoyed the experience. One of the main actors was so familiar, but I couldn't put his name to mind. It worried me throughout the film. Finally, at the conclusion, I waited eagerly for the credits. As they began to roll, so did the audience. They apparently didn't share my curiosity. As I sat studiously watching the screen, the people seated directly in front of us rose to leave. In my frustration, I shouted, "Sitzen sie!" And by God, not only the couple in front of us, but the entire audience stopped and sat back down. I never felt such power. I was so overcome that I forgot the credits, and soon the crowed regained their composure and filled out, leaving me wondering if that was the German psyche or might I be a leader of men?

# Chapter LIV

# Fool Me Twice . . . .

OUR SECOND SEASON with Franz Althoff came to an end, but he booked his entire show into the Palais des Sports, a massive arena in the heart of Paris. The show got in early, and we had plenty of time to adjust and practice in these new surroundings. Across the street was a café, and I remember a sign in white wash on the front window announcing "Today, cous cous." We had to go and see what that meant. A new experience and another menu Mary learned and perfected. The Morrocan influence was very strong in France.

Our show didn't open for another week so I was not concerned over Roger's late arrival. Mary and I felt out the rigging, and everything looked promising. Coming down from our practice, Herr Althoff asked where our other flyer was. I assured him he would be here shortly. "Well, I hope you're right, but I just saw him across town at Cirque d'Hiver, flying to the Alizas." I couldn't believe this was happening again. With fear and doubt, Mary and I caught the metro out to the other circus, and the ugly truth was there before our eyes. Roger, the young child we had taken from San Antonio and taught to be a professional, had left us and joined up with the enemy. "Fool me once, shame on you. Fool me twice, shame on me." He had done it again, and we opened next week.

The Laribles, teeter board act, was on the bill with us; and they came to me and said their boys had some experience and would be happy to fill in for the two weeks. I was skeptical but desperate. Two huskey acrobats and their sister went up, and I still can't believe they were able to fill in and do so with such success. Of course, they were gymnasts and experienced performers, plus I still had Mary carrying the act. In order to beef up the performance, Mary had decided to present her 2 1/2 salto while blindfolded and with a sack over her head. There was a hush in the packed arena as Mary sat on the second raise, a black sash covering her eyes, and slipped the gunny sack over her blonde head. But damn her, when she mounted the raise and groped blindly for the trapeze, she stopped, waved her hand at the spotlight, and shouted, "Damn it! Turn off that light. I can't see!" Fortunately, she spoke no French. Despite minor errors, Herr Althoff was pleased with our presentation. At the end of our engagement, I tried to pay the kids for their life-saving help; but Benito, their boss, refused and said it was their duty as fellow performers and he relished the experience I had given his kids. I blessed them, each and every one, and in the same oath cursed Roger Mireles for having screwed me again.

# Chapter LV

# Cliff Robertson Learns
# The Ropes

BEFORE FATE DEALT me the royal flush of circus life, my dream had been fame as a movie actor. I did excel in the school plays, and my major at the university was speech and drama. I did well and entertained the thought of furthering my education at the Pasadena Playhouse in California. I've often wondered how life might have been if I had gained my Actors Guild union card. I had talent, I was good looking enough, and my body was a definite asset. I could have ended up a star, a druggie, an alcoholic. They all seem to go hand in hand in that festering film land. Thankfully that profession eluded me, and the gods led me down the path of the circus. Here a clean life was a prerequisite; and, ironically, I ended up making more films with major companies and working with their stars. Only last week I read of a close and dear friend, Cliff Robertson, passing away. Funny, we hadn't seen each other in, come, has it been forty-three years?

"The Big Show."

We were in Munich, and they were shooting *The Big Show* with Cliff, Ester Williams, and Robert Vaughn. Cliff was the flyer, and I was pleased at how readily he listened to my instructions and suggestions. We spent late nights in his hotel suite as he ran over his script, and his attention was rapt as I revealed various flying incidents, and he was eager to hear more of circus lore and particularly the past histories of flyers and catchers and all aerialists. He wanted to feel the emotions, thrills, and fears that made up this unique group of entertainers. No pun, he wanted to throw himself into the roll. Meaningless to most but most significant to me was the scene of the deserted, darkened circus ring. He and Ester enter, hand in hand. Overhead is the cold steel flying trapeze rigging. The bar hangs dead. There is no audience, no action, only this silent, beautiful arena. She looks impressed, and Cliff says, "This is where I work." The director says, "Cut! It's a wrap." And they all went their way. But I stayed, long after, absorbed in this setting; of this still scene and the wonderful acknowledgement that, yes, this is where I work.

Not every day was as romantic. This particular scene called for Cliff (Walter Long was doubling) to do a double salto to me, and I was to lose him; let him slip from my grasp and fling him into the apron (high extension of the front of the net). The shot was explained, cameras (four different angles) were loaded, set up, and we all took our places. I sat motionless in the catch bar as the director strode into the ring and enthused over the drama required. Fifteen minutes passed, and he continued to stress the emotions desired, the violence and danger of the shot. Twenty-five minutes dragged by, and my buttocks ached from the cold steel bar

LEE STATH (MARILEES)

on which I sat. Suddenly, he turned and shouted, "Roll 'em." And the cameras started to whir. I began, frantically, trying to build up a swing from a dead stand still. To get a swing up to the required height would take two or three minutes, maybe more. But after a few feeble efforts and only a minimal arc achieved, he jumped from his chair, shouting, "Cut! Cut! Cut!" while jumping up and down, flinging his script on the ground. Cursing and pointing a shaking finger directly at me, he spewed, "You idiot! Do you have any idea the amount of film you cost me?" That was the beginning of a very poor friendship.

Part of my job was, I don't know, technical director? I'm not sure. We all had impressive titles, though our contribution might be small. In one of the scenes, the girl flyer was to be shown in a close up, standing on the board with the trapeze in hand, preparing to swing off for her trick. This young attractive starlet pointed out vociferously that there was no way she was going to climb all the way up that ladder and teeter forty feet off the ground. That was not in her contract. With surprising calmness and guile, the director soothed the outraged actress and called a halt to the day's shooting. A crew of workers and a backhoe worked through the night and excavated a fifteen-foot hole, deep enough in which to place the cameras. Next morning, the trapeze board was placed safely at the edge of the hole; and Ms. Prima Donna took her place, smiled, and took hold of the trapeze. Now it was my turn. Here is where I excelled. No flyer would hold the bar snug against their chest (or ample bosom in this case). It was all wrong. One must lean out, stretch away from the board, and be at arm's length. I was quick to step in and point out this grievous error. I took the proper position, arching my back and leaning far out. "Like this. See?" "Silence!" cried the ogre. "You . . . what's your name? Aren't you the one that sat on the trapeze like a turd and cost me thousands of dollars in wasted film? Listen, Mr. Catcher, I'm making this film for millions of enthralled patrons, and I don't give a damn if a few of you circus clowns snicker. Now get off my set." I managed to keep a low profile until they finished the film. Yet I was sorry to see the end of that profitable fantasy. I never worked so long, did so little, and got paid so much. I lost a lot of my envy and wonder for the film industry through that experience.

"Cliff in the spotlight (note light man in foreground)

Still so many interesting people were met and friendships made. It was some years later, in 1968, and we were working in Dusseldorf. We had just finished the act on an unusually hot day; and I remember standing outside our trailer, my leotard top pulled down, letting the sun and faint breeze cool and dry my body, when Herr Kummel, the publicity director, ran over. Yes, in that heat and over the stubbled lot on which we parked and with his sizable paunch, he breathlessly gasped that someone of importance wanted to see us. I was agreeable but not about to trudge back into the sweltering tent. "I'll bring them out." And he was gone. I assumed it was some agent or circus director, but in our

LEE STATH (MARILEES)

disheveled state, I was ill-prepared to be greeted by Cliff Robertson and his lovely wife, the millionaires Dina Merrill, picking their way through the field to come pay us a visit. Fortunately, our caravan was new and tidy, and we greeted them warmly, offering the limited hospitality of our "home." They seemed entranced by the simplicity and accepted our surroundings with genuine joy. I'm sure it was the novelty of the setting, but we were at home and they were our guests. Naturally, the circus seized the publicity opportunity, but Cliff and Mrs. Robertson were most gracious and accepted the intrusions. After the photo ops, we could ease into our humble surroundings and talk of old times. What nice people. I miss you, Cliff.

"Greeting Cliff after so many years."

# Chapter LVI

# Las Vegas And Circus Circus

WE FINISHED THE 1968 year successfully, but with Blackpool already booked for the coming season and being one flyer short, I thought we must return to the States and find that ever elusive flyer. In retrospect, I'm impressed at how cool we accepted these ever occurring hardships. We got in touch with Nacho Ibarra, that flamboyant flyer who had helped us out in Mexico some years earlier, and reached an agreement for his partnership for the coming season.

That done, Mary and I took our leisure and drove casually out west, enjoying the country over which we had dashed, pell-mell, without appreciation in the past. Like tourists, we took it all in and arrived eventually in Las Vegas. This was not by chance for we had long heard of the fabulous Circus Circus, an exotic casino that provided nonstop, twenty-four-hour circus entertainment. We looked forward to greeting old friends and seeing new acts. What a Mecca of circus acts. There was a permanent flying trapeze rigging set sixty feet above the casino floor, and with four different acts employed, there was a flying act performing every two hours. It was the nearest thing to Nirvana we could wish for.

The first day, we almost spent the full twenty-four hours watching this spectacle, home again with old friends, talking tricks, exchanging anecdotes, and drinking into the wee hours. Al Dobritch was manager of the show. He was an ex-performer and an old acquaintance. When he heard we were visiting, he called me into his office to talk and he seemed unusually pleasant. As it turned out, one of his flying acts, the Caverettas, was due two weeks' vacation. Would the Marilees fill in for that time? That was perfect for us since laying off for any length of time was murder for our type of act plus, we had a new flyer joining us. I said $1,000 a week would do it, and he quickly said, "Agreed." Back in the '60s, that was top money. With no traveling expenses and the rigging permanently set up, this was a godsend. I phoned Nacho, our flyer in Mexico City, to fly up and bring his jock strap.

While waiting, Fay Alexander, who had long been my idol, asked if I would

"Nacho and the newest Flying Marilees."

fill in and catch his act for a few days. This meant extra money and the pleasure of catching one of the great names in flying trapeze. "What's wrong with your catcher?" I asked. "Oh, he had a little accident, but he'll be back soon." Fay had simplified his routine from the old days, but he was still a joy to catch. He worked so smoothly in the hands he felt like a small child. Also in the act was

SHE FLIES THROUGH THE AIR

Don Martinez, a short muscular phenomena. His tricks were dazzling and a challenge to catch. Toward the end of the act, Don mounted the top raise, slapped his leg and pointed at me. A 3 $\frac{1}{2}$ was Don's big trick, and would I hang for it? Sure! Why not? I'd done it before. Don and Fay exchanged glances. I knew it was different, going to a new catcher. Timing would be questionable, a number of variables. But hey, let's give it a shot. All the time, during the act, I had felt uncomfortable in the strange catch bar. The padding didn't quite fit my legs, but I could boast that no flyer had ever pulled me out of my bar. Still, I was puzzled over the strange white Halloween mask tied to the catch bar cable. Some theatrical gimmick, I guessed. Don was on the top raise, and the ringmaster brought the public's attention to the next attempt of the awesome and rarely attempted 3 $\frac{1}{2}$ somersault to the legs. The tourists held their breath, and I noticed some of the habituate gamblers look up and even the roulette wheel stood still. I pumped up my swing and glanced left into the balcony that was at the same level as our rigging. There was Al Dobritch, and some of his cronies come to watch. At one time, many years earlier before Al immigrated from Poland, he had been a trapeze performer of sorts so his interest was understandable yet gratifying. I sat my swing for what I thought the trick needed, looked over my shoulder, but Don wanted me higher. I kicked it up a bit, but he still wanted more. I hoped he knew what he was doing. He nodded, I dropped down into my lock, and he stepped off into space. I was impressed at his powerful force out on the initial swing. As he returned back over the pedestal board, my swing took me forward, and he disappeared from my view. When I reached the far end of

LEE STATH (MARILEES)

my arc, away from the action, the impulse is to duck your head back to get a peek as to what was going on. But I had learned long ago to fight that urge. It alters the pendulum and changes the timing a nanosecond. I hung out there, at the front end, until gravity said it was time to get back and see what was in store for me. My first glimpse was this tiny sequined muscular ball spinning at least twenty-five feet above me. We had a long way to go before we got together. That moment came terribly quick, and the little bastard weighed a hell of a lot. I clamped his open legs and off we went together. Not an easy catch, but we held it and I felt good about it. After the act Fay thanked me, and Don strutted around. Admittedly, it was some trick. Al called me into his office and shook my hand warmly. He seemed eager to talk, like he wanted a friend, but I was sweaty and needed a shower. "Oh, by the way. This is for you," he said and stuffed $1,000 in my dirty, calloused hand. "I had a feeling you could do it, and I made a $10,000 bet with those playboys with me. I made a bundle and kicked some ass, thanks to you. Sit down and have a drink." I thanked him, but I was anxious to get away from this sumptuous office and wealthy apportionment. That massive window overlooking the Vegas Strip seemed ominous and oppressive. I needed a shower. "Oh, one thing, Al. What was that funny white mask tied to the catch bar?" I asked. "That?" he replied. "Didn't they tell you about their catcher?" "Well, yes, they said he'd had an accident" was my simple reply. "Accident, hell," he hooted. "He had an accident every show. That mask is a hard plastic hockey mask that Don's catcher put on for every 3 $\frac{1}{2}$. Don's a hell of a flyer, but he forgets to open his knees on those leg tricks. Thus, the mask to keep from breaking his catcher's nose again and losing any more teeth. But the broken jaw kept him out of this night's show. Doesn't that piss you off?" "No, not really." I sighed. "Fay paid me well, and I knew what a 3 $\frac{1}{2}$ looked like. I've opened a lot of flyers legs, but Don did a good trick. Sure, I've had my nose busted twice. Lost these front teeth and fractured three ribs; but I think, maybe, Don thought my head was a little too hard to mess with." Al liked that and offered a drink again. I promised a rain check and headed for the showers.

Al was out of his league in Vegas. He made a ton of money, gambled too much, and got into drugs. He owed the Mafia money he couldn't pay. So when his death, from a high rise hotel, through a large glass window was listed as a "Possible suicide." One could only wonder, "Why didn't you open the window, Al?"

LEE STATH (MARILEES)

## Chapter LVII

# Catching Hell

**W**E DID OUR two weeks, and even though our last show was at 5:00 AM, it was a heady experience. That time of the morning and there were actually crowds in the casino watching and gambling. The motel, in which we had booked, already came with the windows sealed with tin foil so no daylight would enter. Work all night and sleep all day. The Silver Slipper, that casino down the strip, had a buffet crammed full of every edible element known to the American palate; and this was ours for $1.99.

With time on our side, we hung around. The Flying Far Fans catcher approached me and asked if I would catch his act for a few shows. He had a bad shoulder. I relished the challenge, and the extra money was welcomed. After a few performances, I understood why he had a bad shoulder. Armando, his brother, outweighed me by twenty-five pounds. Big tricks but HEAVY! I kept them in the air, and on payday, each flyer said they had enjoyed working with me. Now the Caverettas were back, Terry asked if I could hang for them for one show. I seemed to be in great demand. This was a pleasurable experience. Beautiful, petite young ladies and executing first-class tricks. I enjoyed that show.

In the dressing room, after my shower, Mary cornered me and asked what the hell did I think I was doing? "I was just filling in for the Caverettas," I answered. "You bastard! I saw you catching that cunt. I know what you're up to." She turned on her heel and left me standing there with the knowledge that, "Here we go again." Mary didn't like me fraternizing with the enemy (females).

LEE STATH (MARILEES)

# Chapter LVIII

# The Beginning Of The End

BACK TO BLACKPOOL, and to us it was like coming home again. Our trailer and truck were waiting at the winter quarters and friends, from five years previously, welcomed us back. I joined the Stanley Park golf club for the year for a paltry 68 pounds, roughly $100; and at the end of our engagement, they refunded me 28 pounds. Oh, how I tortured those lush fairways. But enough about golf.

We were half way through the season and Nacho was a real ball of fire. He ignited a competitive spirit in Mary that our other flyers had not wished to see in her. Midsummer and we were doing three a day. Second show and the attendance was a bit sparse. Mary put up the raise for her trick, and Nacho teased her, asking, "Are you going to do another girly trick? Put up the third raise and catch that triple." Mary signaled me. and I adjusted my swing for that trick. As she backed up over the pedestal board, Nacho shouted, "Break full." She came down the hill and did indeed break full and hard. I was at the far end of my swing, but I heard it. It was like a pistol shot. It was her right shoulder dislocating. The audience gasped; the orchestra stopped, and as I swung back, I saw her writhing in the net. Unable to move, we could only slack off the net and, once again, pick up this broken body.

At St. Anne's Hospital, I held her wrist, trying to comfort her and ease her pain. "Don't! Please don't touch me. I can feel your pulse pounding all the way up into my shoulder. Leave me alone." How can you turn loose of someone so dear? I was desperate to help her. I wanted to share her pain. Shortly thereafter, after heavy sedation, the doctor was able to relocate the shoulder in its socket. "Interesting," he said to me. "In all my years, I've never seen a dislocation in this manner. It's as if the arm had been wrenched out of its joint. Very unusual." Oh, my sweet Mary. You have always been very unusual. I waited anxiously to hear our future from the doctor. The circus seemed as anxious as I. When the doctor finally addressed me, he said, "She's doing fine. Plenty of rest. Intensive therapy and she should be okay in perhaps a year's time." "Can she fly again?" I persisted. This doctor was one of those rare gems you pray for in hospitals. He actually put his arm around my shoulder and led me out to the corridor. "I've seen your act work, and you don't want to put her through that kind of stress. Her shoulder will not hold up to that kind of punishment. Be quite happy. She is healthy and with time can lead a very normal life." A normal life! Who the hell wants that?

So we were finished. Out of business. Closed for repairs. I sold our beautiful trailer and prepared to return to the States to join the unemployed line in an unemployable status. Could I resume a role as school teacher? Was there any demand for the old-fashioned, heavy, deep sea diving profession I had mastered? Not likely. There had

LEE STATH (MARILEES)

been startling advances in that field, and my twenty-year absence had left me out of the loop as lightweight scuba divers darted around where I had previously plodded in the murky depths. No. I was a good trapeze catcher with no one to catch.

# Starting Over Again

**W**E PONDERED OUR fate in London, when out of the blue (though the day was cold, damp, foggy, and drear) came an old acquaintance from South Africa. It was Keith Anderson, the same scroungy youth we had befriended back in Durban so many years ago. He had been in to see our agent and learned of our misfortune. So there in the fall months, in the year 1969, Keith asked if we had no other engagement, why didn't we fly down to Cape Town and see what he had done with our old net. We didn't have any future, and the glowing picture he painted of his promising trapeze school sounded better than teaching a normal school. He boasted of twenty-four eager youths all asking to be instructed in the art of flying trapeze. They waited only for the Messiah's return. I couldn't say no.

I'm forty-three years old now and never in better shape. "Bring it on and take us back to Africa," I cried. Upon our arrival, Keith made arrangements for us to stay at a friend's house, Anthony Clark, who was a cousin of Arthur C. Clark, the renowned fiction writer. Anthony owned a large bookstore in the Cape and welcomed us into his home as family. We were given full run of his typical South African estate. His wine cellar was extensive, and the black servants were attentive to our every need. Tony was a man of slight build, soft spoken, and a well-read individual. His personal library was vast, and long after Mary had retired, I sat in his heavy leather chair, listening to a choice of classical music on his stereo player. Browsing through his books, I came upon Ernie Pyle's account of the battle of Monte Casino. A grisly recall of that siege and in that lengthy narrative was a reference of one "Lt. Anthony Clark" and his heroic actions leading his command up that fortified mountain, the casualties sustained, and his repeated, relentless pursuit of duty for his king and the men in his platoon, a real-life hero. I could only marvel at this small unassuming man and the courage he displayed in that awesome massacre. At dinner, the next evening, I asked him about the four sieges of Monte Casino and the merits he received in the book. Characteristic of a true hero he dismissed it and brought our attention to the extraordinary meal Mary had brought to the table. As to his exploits in battle, he passed those over as accidents of circumstance. He preferred to talk of his relationship to his cousin, Arthur. "Now there was a true hero of literature and not just by accident."

That was the good part. Now I had to earn my keep. Our reputation had preceded us and now confronted by two score of eager young healthy youths, I was forced to push my forty-three years of clean living against teenage gung ho. A few hours of calisthenics and I had spotted the most athletic of the group. He was aggressive and rose to every challenge. A blond Dutch lad, named Larry, whose twin brother, Ronnie, caused me no ends of consternation, trying to differentiate between the two. Larry wanted to prove himself, and so far, he had. "How old are you, Larry?" I asked. "Nineteen, sir," he replied. I liked that "sir" bit. "OK, gang, let's all do chin-ups and try for your max." The troupe gathered around the four bars Keith had set up, and they did more than they had believed possible. Keith whispered to Mary, "They're responding as I had wished. They seem inspired." "Probably because of your hype and propaganda," Mary replied. Larry had waited until the gang had finished and then openly challenged me. The kid was strong, and he had the support of all his friends. *Show the old man*, they were thinking. We each jumped up to the bars, and the kids started counting. A glorious hot sunny day and I was in my element. No cheating; all the way up to the chin and a full extension down. So we went, side by side, Larry muscling himself effortless up, while I swung rhythmically and with tempo from years of experience beside him. At the count of forty, I noticed him struggling and I admired his ability to continue to the count of forty-five before he dropped gasping to the ground. I continued to fifty and eased down, saying, "I always try to do ten more than my age, but you, Larry, I think you far exceeded that today. Well done." But could there be any doubt? I was the alpha male. Now we could start training to be trapeze artists.

A more motley bunch I have never seen. Circus performers were an elite group of physical perfection. I was presented a mélange of misfits: gawky, skinny teenagers with shaggy, unkempt hair. This was my first encounter with what became known as "hippies." Most surprising to me was their relishing the label of "hippies." What was I to do with these rebellious "wannabe" flyers? Mary was there and brought me quickly to my senses. "Get off your ass and quit whimpering. It wasn't too long ago that I was presented with the same scenario. But YOU were the misfit. A 'First of May,' a 'hippie' before your time." Me, like that? I wondered, *Is that really the way she saw me those many years ago?* Damn, I always thought I was a natural. So she really was my Svengali. My pride crushed and put in my place emphatically, I turned to the task of metamorphosing these eager, lost South African children. Keith had gathered this group of orphans, rejects, and loners and was trying in his way to give them something of value, a purpose or goal in life. They needed a family and strict guidance. Strict, I could be. The father figure was not my bag. They could never be my kids. But hell, they went ahead and made me their daddy anyway. Their first cunning move was to address me as "master." Well, bless you, my children. I was theirs immediately. It was only later that I learned "master", in Afrikaans, was a term for any teacher. Yet I relished the anointment each time I was so addressed.

## Chapter LX

# I've Got An Idea

THE ACTUAL BIRTH of our coup began when I was relating stories and history of the flying trapeze to my new partner, Keith Anderson. I told him of the great acts I had seen and the legends of which I had heard. This piqued his imagination and innovative character, and when I told of the Ward-Bell Flyers and their triple wide act, he jumped up, shouting, "That's it. We'll do it. We'll build a double wide act, and you can be the first ever seen in Europe." And that was the beginning of the Marilee Flyers.

I loved the idea: two catchers, side by side, and two flyers, doing synchronized tricks side by side. What a novelty. We could pretty well take over the circus world.

It was now 1970. The year had just begun, and in late January, the summer was at its height: practice, two times a day, early morning and again late afternoon. What a glorious setting, there at Kloof Neck with Lion's Head in the distance. This was

"The Ward-Bell Flyers."

Africa once again. Mary and I felt a kinship and familiarity that said we belonged. The daily workouts and grind were, to me, a joy. A little step forward, an awkward swing, the first trick caught. The entire crew was celebrant. Everyone was supportive, and it was infectious. We might possibly make something of this miserable mélange.

Keith, the perennial showman, would sense the inevitable decline of enthusiasm as I hammered at the stalled progress. One early spring morning as I struggled to motivate this gang of sleepy, sore, and complaining youths to stretch, exercise, study the photos (we had no video back then) of last week's mistakes, and GET WITH IT, Keith staggers up and collapses on a bench. He was a frightening mess. His eyes were dark and hollow. The man was ill. In a hoarse, raspy voice, he shouted words of encouragement, inciting the kids to soldier on and tough it out. If he could rise from his death bed to be there for their practice, he expected a reciprocal effort on their part. They girded their loins and worked like Trojans. Mary, ever suspicious, sat with Keith, consoling and mothering as best she could. She stroked and patted him, much to his objections. Then in a stage whisper, she said, "It's makeup! Theatrical makeup! You phony. You're no sicker than I am." He hushed her and quickly repaired the smeared makeup to his sallow face, and practice continued. So this was my new partner in showbiz, a better showman than I.

Soon the days became weeks, and the weeks became months, and the ugly ducklings were becoming flying trapeze novices, a giant step forward. As we tended to the shaping of the art, Keith was busy with Roberto Germains, our London agent, seeking bookings for our onslaught into the circus world. Keith's financial output seemed unlimited as he had half a dozen riggings welded and assembled: six nets woven. Fanciful costumes with capes to fit the entire ensemble. The moment to lose our juggernaut on the unsuspecting theatrical empire was at hand. With so much raw talent, I could see the framework for six, perhaps seven, trapeze acts.

The world was our oyster. I split up the congregation, leaving Keith to outfit and supply each team; while I siphoned off, what I thought, the most talented and presentable five of the group. I signed a contract to open in Germany, and we called ourselves the "Marilee Flyers."

# Chapter LXI

# The Invasion Of Europe

"We were prepared to fight on the beaches.
To fight on the land . . ."

ONCE AGAIN, ON the Union Castle Line, we were bound for England, that glorious slow passage up the Atlantic, over the Equator, through days of sunshine, squalls, light breezes, and storms. Each morning, before breakfast, I had my reluctant charges topside for pushups, sit-ups, and chin-ups while the puzzled passengers could only wonder at the Machiavellian master that pressed his children to the breaking point. Then they were on their own until the evening ordeal was repeated. Two weeks at sea and we were combat ready.

Our arrival in Southampton was two days late as we had to lie at anchor, in the Sound, as the infamous English fog settled in and chocked off any attempts at sailing into England on schedule. We lay, hove to, with our foghorn belching our presence to any foolish mariner who might chance a landing. Two days and two nights, the provisions were growing low, and tempers were growing high as we stared into the blank wall of gray cotton wool. But all good things must come to an end, and one misty morning, we docked in Southampton and there began a new beautiful experience for the "Marilee Flyers."

Carl Althoff was, without doubt, the worst circus I had ever worked on. Carl Althoff, the patriarch, was the father of Giovanni and Corty; they were his sons and henchmen. You hear Mafia, and you think Napoli. But there, on Circus Althoff, we had the next best thing. The old man, his two sadistic sons, and a crew of German-Moroccan thugs ruled the circus with a vicious iron hand.

Still, we had a contract for our new act, and six young South African kids were to perform in a new strange world called Europe. We opened in Essen, Germany, a massive arena with dressing rooms, running hot water, and toilets. I gathered the group and told them to work their best and enjoy their introduction to the world of circus. Unfortunately, this was going to be the highpoint of the season. After ten days of warmth, dry clothing, hot water, and toilets, they were flung, all six of them, into the back of a rigging truck, pulling one small living trailer that was home for the girl flyer and designated as the cooking and dining area. Mary and I had about the same accommodations. Yet our biggest blessing was that we had never had children.

LEE STATH (MARILEES)

How could we afford to? One pregnancy and one lost season of work. Still, there seemed to be something about us that induced a father-mother image for these young, lost children thrust into a harsh parentless world. How often, late at night, once Mary and I had nestled in bed, were we roused out to mediate between the group and determine why the dishes had not been washed or why hadn't Sandra cleaned all the wardrobe as assigned; and why was Allen, Big Al, the other catcher, trying to get in bed with Sandra after she had already said no? Come on, fellows, I had the same problems at home. So it went pretty much each day, but that was the good part.

Moving day and the hassle of getting up our rigging. Through clever negotiation on my part, the show agreed to transport our rigging. That meant we waited, impatiently, on the circus lot, anxious for the truck to bring our rigging. It never failed. By Corty's orders, our wagon was always the last to arrive. Then the scramble began, getting the iron stakes driven and the rigging erected before the afternoon show. I still question their motive, as the act was good and well received by the public. One of their variety of tricks, Althoff's henchmen would remove the canvas covers we placed on each iron stake to protect the public from shin and foot injuries. Then I was called into the office and harangued by Carl over this negligence. Nine months of this shit, yet we persevered and succeeded. Finally, on one hectic put-up day, we got the rig guyed out and ready for work when Althoff ordered the tent slacked off. That meant doing the whole rigging over again and only thirty minutes before showtime. I was ready for a confrontation. I called my motley crew of six gangly youths together and faced off against Corty, Giovanni, and his Moroccan mob. We were finally prepared to fight. There had been a rumor of how Corty and Giovanni, with his crew, had beaten one working boy to death and tossed his bloody body into the Rhine River and never faced a judge. With this in mind, Big Al, my other catcher, and I stepped forward, backed by our skinny boys, ready for a showdown. For some reason, which I still don't understand, Corty called off his gang. Amazed and relieved, we returned victoriously and jubilant to our trailers. We relished the wine and boasts of battles unfought. Still, life was no better on Circus Carl Althoff.

I should have drawn a distinction between the two Althoff circuses for which I have worked. Carl Althoff was referred to, derisively, as "Schmuck" Althoff, a word I never translated successfully except to know it was unflattering. He was an asshole. Then there was the venerable Franz Althoff, with whom we spent two pleasant years back in the sixties.

From Carl's cruel circus, we escaped to Spain. When I say "escaped," I mean that literally. It was a cold and rainy day when we closed the season in Germany. A dozen performers stood outside the office wagon, waiting to be admitted and receive their final wages. This was a dreaded moment for all. A few of the favored artists entered and came out with their pay envelope and a look of relief. The act before me was contracted in Sweden for the coming year, and once inside, we heard the yelling and cursing. The door opened, and when they exited, their money was hurled out into the mud and rain; but they were pleased to have been paid and set free. My turn came, and I was apprehensive over receiving the two months' pay held back. This was an Althoff

LEE STATH (MARILEES)

gimmick to assure extra leverage in future negotiations. "Well, are you coming back next season?" asked or rather demanded Schmuck Althoff. "It would be an honor, sir," I replied. With that lie, I was given our hard-earned Deutsch marks, and I fled the grounds. The only way Althoff would let us go, pay us the money earned, was when I signed a contract for the next season and promised to return. We loaded up our rigging in an old bus but left our empty rigging truck on Althoff's winter quarters as a sign of sincerity and snuck off, never to return again.

# Chapter LXII

# Land Of The Eternal Fiesta

WE NEVER PAUSED or looked back until we reached Spain where we joined Feijoo-Castilla, an old established, respected dynasty. After a few weeks into our engagement, I was called into the director's office. After some praise and Spanish diplomacy, Mr. Castilla said he would like to make some suggestions. I was open to constructive criticism but not to the outrageous idea he proposed. He said he would like to see each flyer do a trick individually. When one trick was caught, the second flyer would already be in the air preparing to execute the next trick even before the first flyer had returned to the platform. Ridiculous! There would be no opportunity for the first flyer to receive acclaim for his effort. It would be a continuous, uninterrupted thrashing of human bodies. We would look like a bunch of mosquitoes gone mad. I said no emphatically.

We argued long and hard, and in the end, we did it his way. What a stroke of genius. True enough, as I predicted, there was no time for individual praise; but with this bewildering action, this constant flailing of callow youths hid the many faults my young group still possessed. The only pause was for the final trick, the double passage. This was an awe-inspiring trick that all flying acts use and is, in reality, quite simple. But with the Marilee Flyers and six bodies bunched closely in the air together, it was a winner. Only then, at its completion, was the act ready to accept the audience's approval. A unique idea was born.

We prospered and enjoyed two harmonious years with Sr. Castilla in Spain. He was a true gentleman, and the only conflict I can bring to mind was in Ovieado. A big, American television company came and wanted to film our

"The Marilee Flyers floundering in Spain."

act. I was agreeable, and the financial terms were met. The crew set up and made a preliminary shoot; but the following day, when the actually film was to be made, Sr. Castilla asked what was his percentage. I can see now my naivety in not having consulted him in the negotiations. I explained that the contract had been made, and there was nothing in it relating to him. Mary pointed out the lack of diplomacy on my part, and when the evening show opened, Mr. Castilla called me into his office and said he would not supply the lights for filming. I pleaded my case, but he was an old experienced businessman and that was that. I explained my situation to the film director; and he took me aside, gave me the payment in full and said, "Keep it quiet, but I got enough yesterday during the rehearsal. It's in the can." I kept that secret within myself until the end of the season and, only then, told the group and paid them their share.

## Chapter LXIII

# There's A Dog On My Train

STILL ON GOOD terms with Sr. Castilla, we agreed to four weeks in Portugal. Mary and I drove to Germany to check on another contract and left our truck at the Krone winter quarters in Munich. While there, Mary reasoned that it would be cheaper to buy this cute Opel GT than pay the cost of tickets by rail to Portugal and back again. It was a tiny yellow sports car with a black racing stripe, and she did look cool behind the wheel. So off we sped and opened at Coliseu dos Recreios in Lisbon, another dream engagement. The kids parked their outfits in a beautiful park, while Mary and I had the big hotel for a month. This was the land where the lovely Mateus Rose wine was brewed and which made every evening meal a pleasure. The only sour note I could find during that date was the lady announcer. When we missed a trick, she did little to cover the blunder. Instead, in Portuguese, she would whimper, "Oh, what a shame." Otherwise, the public might never have noticed and thought it was part of the act. What a shame.

On our return, Lutt was held up at the German border on some passport technicality. (Those poor South Africans always had problems at every border.) The rigging came through, and we got it hung at the Krone Circus building in

Munich. But where was our other flyer? Herr Sembach was in a rage. "We open in two days. Where is your other flyer?" What a litany. Did all these directors have the same script?

Lutt was on the border being held up with Dog. Dog was our canine companion and had covered more miles than most humans. With his passport and visa finally in order, but time running short, Lutt booked passage on an express train and got a full ticket for Dog. I'll try and describe Dog.

"Though I've belted and flayed you . . . my long lost love, Dog."

He was a massive black sleek coated beast with malamute eyes. He had adopted us a year before in Blanes, Spain. We had all been to the local cinema, and as we strolled back to the circus, he fell in alongside of us and seemed determined to become part of the troupe. The kids begged us to let them keep him. He would be our mascot, our guardian. He was a beautiful thing, and we couldn't say no. Very quickly, it became apparent whose dog it was. Whenever we built up the rigging and I would pace from one end to the other, checking for height and levelness, the dog was by my side, sitting and waiting for my next move. "Hey!" cried Graeme. "Look who's become the alpha male?" So he was my dog, and we called him "Dog."

Back on the border, he sat proudly upon his private seat until the conductor came through checking tickets. "Das ist verboten," he roared. "No dogs allowed." Lutt was never the most diplomatic of my wards and remained seated, stating simply that the seat was paid for and the dog would stay there. The uniformed conductor said to get him out, but Lutt replied, "You get him out." Dog didn't like drunks or uniforms. There was a low menacing growl. Dog remained seated and seemed to enjoy the rest of the journey. With Herr Sembach still cursing, they arrived. We made the opening, and the act was a success.

LEE STATH (MARILEES)

"Dog in Monte Carlo."

# Chapter LXIV

# Goodbye And Hello

NEARING THE END of this engagement, it was a sad day when Lutt came to me and said he wished to leave as he and Katrina, a beautiful French aerialist, wanted to make a try at forming their own act. I was struck by his forthright honesty and I could not stand in his way of trying to move upward. I remember on closing night (he stayed throughout the entire engagement) and we embraced on the dressing room stairwell. We had tears in our eyes when we said goodbye.

One flyer short, we headed for Copenhagen and Circus Benniweis. At the same time, my partner, Keith, had booked one of our many acts with a smaller circus in Denmark. It proved to be disastrous, and when they were let go, it left a floundering bunch of flyers on the loose. I should have been more sympathetic, but instead, I seized the most likely flyer to fill in my vacancy. She was Jackie Battersby, a professional showgirl from England and a capable flyer who filled in perfectly for the Marilee Flyers.

At the close of our act, I wanted one of our flyers to walk along the top of our rigging to the middle and make a simple dive into the net, a nice finish. I presented the opportunity to each of the boys, but each one refused.

"No way am I going to walk on that thin tubing and dive fifty feet, headlong, into the net." "Hell," said Jackie, "no big deal." And she did it every show. Then to add to our troubles, Fred ripped off the flybar and broke his arm. That greatly impaired our performance. When I phoned Keith and told him of our latest dilemma, he said, "I haven't got a replacement but cut his pay until he comes back to work." That was cruel, but we had learned long ago, "no work, no pay." It was a cruel business.

## Chapter LXV

# Another Stone In My Shoe

DESPITE THE HARSHNESS of the profession, the kids managed to accumulate enough money to purchase their own vehicles and caravans; and we moved, en mass, to our contract in France for 1974 with Cirque Jean Pinder. I Lost my other catcher through the whims and caprice of circus; but Keith, my ever efficient partner, had a new one on our doorstep in time for opening.

This was Trevor, a young officious, intelligent lad that hadn't been with us a month before he was offering advice at how I might better manage the act. If I hadn't been so desperate for a replacement, I would have run him down the road. But by the same token, it's a wonder he didn't catch the next plane back to South Africa on his own. The poor kid had no shelter and was obliged to sleep on the couch in Irene's trailer. This didn't go down well with Irene's boyfriend. In time, Trevor managed to buy a small panel truck and slept on the floor until he was able, through diligent labor, to make it a home for one. He even had Mary and I in for dinner one evening and surprisingly presented some very enjoyable escargot. But that didn't make me like him any better. He couldn't seem to restrain himself from offering advice and criticism. Despite the fact that there were probably some very good ideas, I could not stomach a bloody first of May telling me that what I had been doing successfully for so many years could be done more efficiently.

Trevor didn't stop there. He even found things that might make the circus run better and he wasn't hesitant to tell the circus director, another one of my failings was not listening to outside advice. The director, on the other hand, found some of his suggestions wise, and at the end of the season, he offered Trevor his own rigging and act if he would stay and work for him.

All Trevor need do was leave the Marilee Flyers and stay on the show, working for himself and Sr. Cristo. What did Mr. Know It All do? He thanked Sr. Cristo, and though it would have been a golden opportunity, he declined. He said his obligation was to see his commitment with the Marilee Flyers fulfilled. They don't make many men like that anymore. So the act was unified (until Irene asked to be let go as she was marrying into the tumbling act).

# Chapter LXVI

# The Postman Never Rings

CHECKING DAILY WITH Keith by phone and telegram was routine; but getting ones mail, on a traveling show, was always difficult. We were never certain where we might be next week, particularly in Spain. With the promise of a four-day stand, we optimistically sent out the town's name, Saragossa I recall, and the poste restante or general delivery address. Oh, how many towns, how many post offices have we pleaded with the clerks to search further, knowing there must be messages, letters, contracts, or some sort of communication hidden in the labyrinth of postal security. So at the local post ofice I stood once again in the lengthy line of patient, expectant citizens. Just ahead of me, an elderly gentleman took his place at the window and received his social security earnings for the month. He took his envelope and moved unsteadily aside. In a blur, some scoundrel snatched the money and was out of the door before the old man could even protest. He stood staring at the door, his mouth half open in some sort of speechless disbelief. Then I, without a thought, was out of the door onto my ten-speed bicycle and in hot pursuit. Not certain in which direction to look, I pedaled in a matrix form of search, up one street, down another, looking for some suspicious person. My diligence brought me upon a desperate and frightened character. It had to be him. I dropped my cycle and grabbed him by his shirt front. He put his hands over his head and beseeched me to let him go. He was a Moroccan, and pleading in Spanish, he was hardly understandable. But he held out the stolen money and only asked to be let go. I snatched the envelope and frisked his pockets. His wallet was nearly bare, but when I pulled out his identity card, he fell to his knees, clutching at me and begging for what seemed like his life. Being a foreigner in Spain and in legal trouble must have been a terrifying aspect. I tossed his wallet and papers on the ground and told him to get lost and back across the straits. I meant Morocco, but at that stressful moment, all I could think of were the straits of Gibraltar. Nevertheless, he took off at a goodly pace in some direction, and I rode triumphantly back to the post office. The old pensioner was seated, surrounded by a sympathetic crowd. He was grief stricken and beyond words. When I returned his desperately needed pesetas, all he could manage was a near-inaudible "Gracias." I felt real good. Mary said there wasn't any mail for us. Ah, well, perhaps Manana.

## Chapter LXVII

# Just Passing Through

TOMORROW CAME AND went. We finished the date and time to move on. Left a forwarding address for the next town and set out, hoping that our accumulated mail might someday arrive at the same place as we. I wonder what bits of postage, addressed to us, might be wandering still, in pursuit of the ever nomadic Marilees? This was a routine jump: me pushing the massive juggernaut of a truck through winding rough roads with Mary following in her little yellow sports car. At the end of the trail, she could hardly wait to tell me of the excitement I had created as I drove through one particularly narrow village. I remembered the town as it was noon. It was tiny and teeming with the locals. But what a sight we must have been: this English truck with its right-hand drive and Dog, my faithful canine companion as codriver, sitting upright where a European chauffer should be. Unfortunately, I could not depend on Dog's insight as whether it was safe to overtake that slow-moving truck ahead or that wagon with its load of hay or cattle. So it meant plodding slowly behind, kilometer after kilometer, until they either stopped or turned off, too risky to chance. But as we roared through this small town at high noon, my powerful exhaust pipes on the "wrong" side, I was unaware of the clouds of dust and debris spewing up from the gutters. It entered every house and shop and blanketed the quaint roadside cafes. It brought irate and wide-eyed citizens out from their lunch or siestas. Mary said she saw one rotund, apron-covered man, his face still lathered in shaving cream, storm out of the barbers, shaking his fists and shouting Spanish oaths at my offending vehicle. I missed all this fun and drove serenely on.

# Chapter LXVIII

# Ask And Ye Shall Receive

SERENITY! STILL IN Spain and I must admit it was one of our favorite countries. But this trip brought us early into Seville. Good! We pulled up behind a carnival structure and fell immediately into an exhausted sleep. Early evening, midsummer, and with all our windows open, it was bearable in our hot tin truck, until the hour of eight when the Chino Teatro, which we had parked directly behind, came to life. This was a vaudeville type of revue with twenty dancing girls, two vociferous comedians, and a five-piece orchestra (whose lack of musical ability was well compensated with sheer volume). I mean the joint was jumping. Our humble home throbbed with the beat. Seville! Big fiesta! Though we had arrived early, the midway was in full swing. That big band and those equally boisterous dancing broads had eight shows to do. Wet with midsummer southern Spanish sweat, we heard the same music, the same jokes, and the same songs until the last show closed at five thirty the next morning. Soon the sun would rise. The day would begin, and the heat of the night would be replaced by the heat of the day. If only the circus would hurry up and lay out the lot so we could find our allotted space and get some peace. Even with the five shows daily, it would be a madness with which we were familiar.

Be careful for what you ask. The show came in, set up, and we were assigned a spot near the owner's deluxe wagon. This, in itself, was some sort of honor. You could always tell how an act was rated by the position in which one's outfit was parked. Some acts, in disfavor, would wait hours until the layout boss would signal them to park their rigs. "Here!" I can't say we were always in the front row. On some occasions, when a contract renewal was in question, we could be left to fume and wait until, at long last, the word was given to, "put it over there" But here in Seville, we were on the favored list. Near the boss's outfit, we were certain to get a good electric hookup, even better, a hose connection for running water. The caste system was strong on a circus lot. Of course, back in the '70s in Europe, there weren't any flush toilets or holding tanks. We all had our own little portable donniker, and emptying them could be problematic. It was during that first night in Seville, parked too near Angel Cristo's caravan, that his boy or servant carried the noxious waste out and dumped it under our humble home. Good God O'Mighty! I was out and on Angel's doorstep, still retching, and in poor Spanish profanity made it clear that our act wouldn't take that kind of shit. I was soothed and placated and promised the respect we deserved. Come to think of it, maybe that was it.

# Chapter LXIX

# Mary And The White Slave Market

YOU SAY YOU'RE displeased with the sanitary conditions? Be patient. We are opening in Morocco in two weeks' time. Despite the ship grounding, on our short passage across the Gibraltar Strait, we entered a new sphere in Tangier. Despite ten years of traveling the world, we had to admit that here was a new experience. I had a woman dentist give me a root canal that took four visits to her office. On each occasion, after extensive drilling and probing, she would dab a q-tip, bring it to her nose, and sniff saying, "Pas encore," not yet. Finally, success and with the cavity filled, it cost the equivalent of $20.

Mary's experience was not so pleasant, if you can call a root canal pleasant, but certainly more exciting. She had gone to the American Embassy for a visa renewal. Normally, she would have made the excursion on her bike, but

"A romance blossoms in Rabat, Morocco."

I was hesitant to let her try it in this somewhat primitive country. A fellow artist drove her to town and dropped her off. There in the city center, she was thinking how silly I was to worry. It was a teeming metropolis; and once in the embassy, her business concluded, she caught a taxi back to the circus. Mary was very good at directions. We could return to a once visited town, and she could retrace her way to any of the previous spots where we had worked, parked or eaten. In the taxi, she gave the driver explicit directions to the circus. We were always suspicious of taxis taking the long expensive scenic route tour to our destination. So at the very first wrong turn, she was definitely aware that the driver was not heading for the show. She shouted for the driver to stop. She banged on the glass, but he didn't answer or look around. When he made a sharp turn at a corner, Mary had the door open and was out of the cab, rolling on the ground. The taxi never even slowed. She was able to get a ride home, but it would appear that she just missed being caught up in the white slave trade.

Casablanca. How we looked forward to that. We were disappointed that we never found Rick's bar, but Nickstadt appeared again to take us to the other exotic nightspots and best restaurants. It was in one of these really real Moroccan restaurants that the owner, having recognized us from the show, insisted that we dine as his guests. What a treat. I've always loved lamb but done as they do in Morocco was a special experience, right up to the end when the owner proudly presented me with the ultimate honor. It was the lamb's eyeball. I'm pleased to say I was able to show my gratitude by swallowing it whole and make gestures of great delight. In comparison, the root canal was more fun.

At the end of our Moroccan adventure, everyone was burdened with great wads of dirham (the local currency). I knew we would take a beating at the exchange rates back in Spain, but what was one to do? Trevor

"King Saud of Arabia pays us a visit."

had the answer. At the dockside, as we prepared to board our ship, a bearded shifty-eyed rascal approached Trevor and asked if he wanted to exchange dirham for pesetas at a much better rate. Ever suspicious, Trevor asked to see the pesetas first. The Moroccan reached nervously in his plastic bag and disclosed a considerable amount of pesetas. The deal was done, but the bearded one acted hastily and whispered, "Hurry, I'm being watched." A quick exchange was made, and he hurried off. Only on board, as we cast off, did Trevor see the sad drama unfold as he peeled off the top peseta notes only to find a stack of worthless paper. His entire month's wages were somewhere back in Morocco.

LEE STATH (MARILEES)

# Chapter LXX

# Gotta Make It Run

WITH THE PLEASANT Moroccan climate forgotten, we were making a long jump in our old diesel truck. It was in this mobile domicile that we moved across the Italian countryside on a miserable, cold, winter day. Intermittent snow flurries and our slow progress did nothing to enhance the legendary beauty of Italian fields, now lying bleak and bare, mirroring our state of mind. At least the heater in the cab was giving out warmth, actually more than usual. With our normal winter traveling wear of sweaters, heavy jackets, and a blanket apiece to fight the elements and cold drafts that fingered their way through every crack and misaligned door, we were uneasily comfortable. I say uneasily because we both knew this was not the norm. A quick check of oil pressure, always a concern, and all was normal; but the temperature gauge needle was lost, only to appear in the uppermost range, RED! Boiling water was giving us warmth at a high price. I had a perpetually leaking radiator and had long ago given up replenishing it with expensive antifreeze. Instead, I would drain it on freezing nights, and as long as the motor was running on the road and I kept it topped up with water, no need to worry. Such was my warm weather theory. The road was free of traffic and I found a wide shoulder on which to settle and prepared to face my enemy. I sent Mary into the back of the truck, opened the hood to let the steaming radiator cool, and pulled my box of tools from the possum belly. With a wave of despair, I climbed into the engine compartment and with the boiling water quickly dissipated into the freezing winter air, I began the search for my troubles. One lone car whizzed by. What was I hoping for, a diesel mechanic on vacation with spare parts and a heart of gold? A black crow settled on a nearby fence post, spoke harshly, and eyed me suspiciously. Not to worry, I was harmless and felt even more useless. Cold was getting bitter, and I didn't have much daylight left. Filled with self-pity, I pried off the water hose, fearful of not finding the problem and more fearful of what I might find and what I could do about it: an old foreign vehicle in a foreign land, stuck on a desolate, barren road with no civilization or living soul in sight except for the solitary crow. Or was it a raven? I bent to the task. Numb hands fumbled with hard cold wrenches. Coming over to the continent, I had refurbished my tool box with metric measures and now I heaved and hammered the frozen bolts, rounding off their corners and slamming my knuckles against every sharp metal piece under the hood. I had already determined the radiator was serviceable so it had to be the water pump. I wrestled and banged at it with bloody frozen hands until I wrenched it, triumphantly, free. "Aha!" I shouted. The bird, startled to see I was still alive, took wing and soared slowly over the fields, flapping once, twice before disappearing in a nearby copse. Still, flushed with victory, I held the treacherous water pump at arm's length and asked the gods of Engines,

LEE STATH (MARILEES)

"Now what do I do?" The show opened on Friday; and as the feeble winter sun dimmed, bringing a close to Tuesday, my panic mounted. "Where do I get an antique English water pump stuck here in limbo?" It was here that Mary, my soul mate and lover, produced another of her miracles. No, she didn't have a Thames-Trader water pump, but she coaxed me back into a different world. We entered the rear of our truck together, and I was overwhelmed, all at once, by warmth. The kerosene stove radiated heat. Both candles and battery lights transformed the gloom of oncoming night into a glowing haven. Through it all permeated the aroma of a simmering roast in wine sauce. The table was set in front of our plush benches. A special expensive Italian wine, which we had been saving for some future occasion, was opened and breathing. So in her many paneled kitchen, on her full-sized, four-burner French stove, she had somehow created a meal fit for a nearly broken, half-frozen, grateful husband. How did she do that? Out there in the middle of an Italian wasteland, how did she know how to heal me? I knew she was a gypsy and a bit of a witch so I shouldn't question her mystical ability to give me sustenance when most needed.

Dinner was exquisite and slowly enjoyed. We savored it all.

We retired to our bedroom suite and held each other for a long time. We savored it all, slowly and exquisitely. We'd worry about the injured truck tomorrow.

"A simple supper in our luxury suite."

Of course, I miraculously found a water pump, healed the old hulk, finished the jump, and opened on time.

That opening was, once again, in Vienna where we had a month's engagement. While I worked in the building's great machine shop welding and building new ratchets for our rigging, those kids were active as well. All the youngsters had spent time and money taking the necessary driver's schooling in order to obtain their driving licenses. This done, they proudly purchased a used and roadworthy Mercedes Benz. With their new driver's licenses and their first car; they were truly proud, and I too could scarcely conceal my admiration over their growth and maturity. We were not a bad family. We had a long jump to our next date so I got a head start. They were excited and looking forward to their first solo excursion. But not even across the Austrian border, they ran headlong into an oncoming truck. The car was totaled. Mary and I were in Madrid, awaiting their arrival, when they got through by phone and told me of their dilemma. "Is everyone all right?" I asked, "Good, but we open day after tomorrow, and you're where?" I would never have thought of it, but they hired a taxi and had him drive them all the way across Switzerland, France, and into Spain, and finally Madrid. The poor kids had

"The Circus Oscar award for The Marilee Flyers."

LEE STATH (MARILEES)

lost their first auto but gained so much respect from me. Perhaps some kind of balance or justice, but the twenty new ratchets I had built during that month in Vienna were left behind on the lot after one late-night teardown. However, on that same closing in Madrid, the Marilee Flyers were voted the winners of the Circus Oscar.

# Chapter LXXI

# Nurture vs. Nature

HOW GOOD WAS I? Who better than I can answer that question? Despite the obvious prejudice, let me say outright, "I was good." The best catcher of all time? Not likely. But in our era, yes, I was good. Physically, I was not what one expected of a catcher. My working weight was only 155 pounds, but I had unusually large hands yet very slender wrists. Of the many flyers I caught, they all remarked of the joy of being able to get their hands around the catcher's wrists. Normally, the catchers were muscular behemoths with arms the size of my legs. There was no chance for the flyer to grip the catcher's wrist, which could instill confidence and help save a bad trick. When a flyer is not confident of holding a trick, they can slip through the hands of the strongest catchers. So despite my weight disadvantage, a flyer could feel my presence, know we were working as one. Second, I was fearless. Others called it foolhardy, but I was never worried about being hit. My reputation was, "Get Lee. He'll hang for anything." And hang I did. I've caught some of the wildest, most innovative tricks thrown and by some who outweighed me by thirty pounds. Oh, yes, the kid was good.

Which brings me to the point of this self-praise. It was with the South African group of Marilees and we had been trying hard for the elusive triple. Graeme and Freddy were both on the cusp of achievement; but despite my experience, instructions, criticism, and long hours of practice, they were unable to produce the trick needed. I was discouraged with them. So one pleasant day in Toledo, Mary and I went into the village where El Greco once lived and painted. An outdoor staircase held a purported original painting, hanging unprotected, on the wall. Fascinating! On our return to the circus, we were met by the whole jubilant bunch with the wonderful news that Trevor, our other catcher, had caught Graeme's first triple. Both Mary and I shouted with joy and pounded their proud backs. "Well done. Bravo!" I cried. They were so excited and elated that one had to share this moment of glory. It was not until Mary and I reached our truck and locked ourselves inside that I broke down. Mary knew it was coming and held me tightly, but I was crushed. Egoist that I was, or am, I knew what this meant. I was no longer the great catcher I once was. Trevor, faithful employee and later closest friend, had usurped my reign and exposed me for what I had become, a "has been." Later in his career, with his own act, Trevor caught the quadruple, a trick I never even looked at.

# Chapter LXXII

# A Royal Performance

HOW GOOD WERE we? The Flying Marilees? I never really knew or suspected. This was back in the late '60s prior to the Marilee Flyers. We had worked with so many prestigious world-class acts that I rarely thought to compare ourselves in a competitive manner. But the first hint of our stardom was brought emphatically before my eyes during an engagement in Brussels in their arena: two full weeks with full houses every show. The act had gone well without one miss. And to go twenty-eight performances in a flying trapeze act with not one miss was quite an achievement. After our two weeks of personal triumph, closing night brought a gala performance with King Albert and Queen Paola present in their royal box seats. Again we climbed up and did an inspired act. (Royalty does that.) Mary was electric, and even with that massive crowd, she seemed to make personal contact with each individual, the signs of a real artist. I was elevated by her performance, and we came down to an ovation from the audience. Then, as we took our last bow to leave, the king and queen both rose from their seats and continued their applause. With the sovereign's nod of approval, the entire arena stood as one and gave us an unending roar of appreciation. I was overwhelmed. As flowers were showered into the ring, I took Mary's hand and presented her to the king and queen and her adoring fans. That's how good the Flying Marilees were.

"Flying Marilees in Brussels."

## Chapter LXXIII

# We Was Robbed

TOUGH ACT TO follow. So how good were the Marilee Flyers? With Mary grounded for good, with her torn shoulder, and me saddled with those inexperienced South African kids, my primary objective was to make an honest living, which brings me to the question I asked earlier, "How good were the Marilee Flyers?"

It was in Monte Carlo, the 1978 Circus Festival, and such a prestigious event is unrivaled in the circus world. Five days of circus entertainment with a completely new program each night. The finest acts in every category, be it lions, tigers, or bears; jugglers, teeter board, single trapeze, clowns, seals, any circus act that could be considered the best from any of the competing countries of the world. They were assembled here to vie for the coveted first place, the Golden Clown. And there we were, the Marilee Flyers, going up against the best in the world.

We arrived early. I was anxious to get my kids acclimated to the pressure of this fairyland. They were terrifyingly intimidated to be in the presence of such great circus luminaries. We got our rigging up and had one satisfactory practice in the empty circus arena. It was a beautiful tent, a blue expanse of canvas brought in by Enos Togni and set up with the help of Eddie Murillo on the vast expanse of beach belonging to the principality of Monaco.I was pleased with the kids practice and confident we could hold our own. Then the news came in that we would be going up against the Flying Gaonas. That meant Tito and his triple. We didn't have a triple on which to rely. My group was petrified. We couldn't possibly compete against that quality. I assembled the wide eyed group in a huddle and threatened them with bodily harm if they didn't pull themselves together and present their very best. Forget the Gaonas. We would do our act, get our money, and leave quietly.

The week was magical. All the celebrities of both circus and filmdom were there to watch this conglomerate of circus talent. Being in the presence of Prince Rainier and the beauty of Princess Grace left this old pro a little awestruck. We watched each performance every night and grew more and more apprehensive as doomsday approached, the night of our execution.

It finally arrived. The orchestra had been through our music. I had keyed the spotlight crew. The net was stretched, and we were in the air. God bless those clumsy kids. They flew like professionals, and I could only take a free breath when we finished the last trick and came down with a clean act. The response was like a tsunami. But why not? For eight minutes, nonstop, there had been this frenetic action of young athletes, flipping, twisting, and somersaulting in the air only to be followed by another. From start to finish, there were no announcements or even applause. There was no time, only a few gasps or a shout. But when it was all over, they let us know. As I rebounded in the net, I saw Princess Grace stand as she applauded.

LEE STATH (MARILEES)

OK, we had made it. Now we could take our well-earned money and leave with pride unblemished. The final night was well worth the price of admission. The Gaonas were flawless, and Tito did his triple to great acclaim. The Fifth Festival

"Cary Grant, Princess Grace, Prince Rainier, Madame Jacqueline Cartier and Princess Stephanie marvel at the Marilee Flyers."

International du Cirque Monte Carlo 1978 had concluded and left only the gala night of award presentations. Such an outstanding event, in that small principality, brought banner headlines out in the early morning editions of the local papers. There were varied revues of the week's entertainment: some praiseworthy, others more candid. One such headline stated boldly, "Marilees were robbed." I questioned my French translation. We had received our money in full. We were awarded the first-place award by the Jury of Radio Monte Carlo and the second-place award of the Silver Clown by the elite selection of judges attending.

As I meandered around the near-deserted circus grounds that next morning, I ran into Sean Connery, one of the judges. Showing him the newspaper, I asked if my interpretation was correct. Always the gentleman and diplomat he replied, "That's the opinion of some." Probing for more details, we were joined by another of the judges, John Ringling North himself, and he was more candid. "Mr.

Marilees, we were up until three in the morning, not an unpleasant hour what with the company and excellent wine, arguing over what we considered the most entertaining act of the festival." "You were a judge?" I asked. "Yes, myself, Mr. Connery here, along with Cary Grant, Telly Savalas, David Niven, and of course Prince Rainier and Princes Grace. It was really a pleasant evening, but our argument with the prince was why he had brought in two such outstanding flying acts to make our decision so difficult." His reply was honest, though blunt, when he said he had no idea the Marilees were of that

"Sean Connery, Lee and the impresario, Mr. John Ringling North."

quality. The argument and final decision went down to Irvin Feld who was now the sole owner of the Ringling Brothers Circus. He pointed out the clause in his contract that the Gaonas were assured of first prize if they were to attend. I was reminded of an incident, earlier in the week, when Mr. Feld and I had had a confrontation over his rights to televise our performance but with no additional payment. I had bluntly refused and could see I had not made a friend of this influential showman. Still, I was elated over our success and the fly we had inadvertently plopped into the ointment. Mr. Connery accepted my challenge for a round of golf and thrashed me soundly. He agreed to a rematch next time we were in Marbella.

LEE STATH (MARILEES)

Now so many years later, I look at our second place silver clown. It's tarnished and dull, and if you don't look carefully, it looks like what it should have been, the Gold Clown.

"Trophies from the Monte Carlo Festival 1978."

# Chapter LXXIV

# Mystery H2O, Machinery, And Mary

DO YOU KNOW anything about diesel engines? I certainly didn't. In my childhood, our family's toolbox contained a hammer, a screw driver, and a pair of pliers. Of these, my mother was usually the only one able to manage their complexity. But now, after nursing, cajoling, and praying that six-cylinder behemoth through a dozen countries; having unattainable parts fashioned and molded by ingenious Spanish and Italian mechanics; easing the improvised parts into place; hammering in the recalcitrant misfits yet always finding a way to patch it together and keep up with the show, I slowly learned. Looking back, I'm amazed at the various trades I mastered.

It was summertime, and I knew I had a leaky head gasket. I needed a large fifty-liter plastic bottle of water to keep the radiator from boiling dry. Then we were blessed with a two-week layoff when the show had to finally replace the rotten canvas tent. There was a lot of grumbling, two weeks without pay. It was not the kind of vacation an artist welcomed. But in my case, I was pleased. Now I could undertake some desperately needed repairs. We found a secluded camping site only a few kilometers from the circus grounds. It had electric hook up, good water, and even hot showers. We picked a private spot among some lush eucalyptus trees. I leveled the old truck on the heavy wooden blocks we carried for that purpose and settled in to repair, not just the truck; but with two weeks, we also hoped to mend some of the tears and strains of our bodies that had accumulated during the grueling Spanish season. Both of Mary's shoulders were in bad shape, and she was unable to lift her arms high enough to curl her hair; I learned another profession: hair dresser. Each night, after the last performance, I would painstakingly roll up and set her hair for the next day's performance. As for me, my thighs were raw and festered where the trapeze bar dug in every show. I had also torn half of my right bicep. So maybe two weeks would give us a chance to heal.

We savored those first few days: sleeping late, eating the best foods available, and browning in the warm Mediterranean sun. But now it was time to take the old truck to the garage and get a new head gasket fitted. I had learned to carry all the spares I thought we might need, tires I could scrounge and find a mate. But gaskets for a foreign make were pushing one's luck.

I leapt out of bed and climbed into the cab to give it a go. Nothing! One "clunk" and nothing more. I'm an optimist by nature and so continued in my effort to coax life into that slumbering beast. "Battery's dead," opined Mary. But I always kept it on trickle charge during our idle time. That shouldn't be the problem. Even so, I put the charger on "FULL" and gave it an hour. "Now, you sumbitch, START!" I cursed. One grunt was the only reply. OK, I'm a practical man, and though I was certain the battery was sound, I went to the garage and asked to borrow a battery to jumpstart the "Muther." I hooked it up, double-checked, and with confidence cranked it again. Another "grunt." Sob, sob. Unless you have tried some time in your life to correct a fault or defect and met failure at each try, then realizing you have no way out, that you are trapped in a corner with no means of escape and you know, for certain, you are going to die then and there; if you have not had that experience, then you cannot understand the tragedy of my situation. Ten tons of recalcitrant truck that had been my home, my life,

my ticket to success was now doomed to stand unmovable, dead, as vegetation crept slowly to cover it and me; and we were all swallowed up by nature.

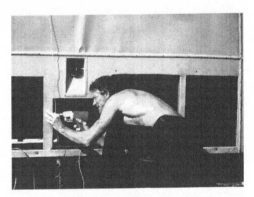

"Looking into the labyrinth."

I took back the borrowed battery and told the mechanic that it didn't work either. "I can't leave the shop now. Tell me, what's your problem?" I told him my sad story and how I had planned to bring the truck in because of a leaky head gasket. "Head gasket?" he queried. "Yeah," I replied. "That much I'm sure of." "Then," he replied, carefully relighting a crumpled, half-used cigarette, "you've got a hydrostatic lock." And he returned to his hiding place inside the hood of an old Pegasus lorry. "Well, what's a hydrostatic lock and how do I unlock it?" I asked. He was a gnarled, angry-looking Spaniard, yet a sympathetic man. He was the kind one often

LEE STATH (MARILEES)

came into contact in those earlier years in Spain; and usually, when you came to the point of desperation with shouts of "Please, help me!" they did. He slowly and painfully eased himself out of his cramped captivity. He stretched his wiry frame. He meticulously wiped his knobby, scarred hands that spoke of many slipped wrenches on old rounded head bolts and peered thoughtfully back into the hood of the old relic on which he had been imprisoned. Then asked, "Got your own tools? "Yes," I replied. "OK, then here's what you have to do. One of your six cylinders is filled with water from your leaking gasket. And there's no way any battery is going to compress that water. Water doesn't compress. So it's called a hydrostatic lock, a water lock." Oh, God," I whimpered, "is my engine ruined?" "No, you go back," he slowly explained, "pull the number one injector and then see if it cranks. If it does, you'll see a fountain of water squirt out. If not, put back the injector and pull out number two and so on until you find the troublemaker." I did not kiss the cuffs of his greasy coveralls, but I did thank him repeatedly and then rushed back to my truck, my home, my sick child with new hope that a cure had been found.

It was late now, though the sun was creating a spectacular show of scrambled colors that mimicked a firestorm among the forest of pine trees. I could hardly wait to test my new found friend's theory, but Mary insisted I come in and have supper and a good night's rest before accepting the challenge. I did as she said. I had a very good meal, but a good night's rest was not easily achieved.

Strange how one boasts "I didn't sleep a wink last night," and when dawn came at last, I was reminded of the ancient Chinese proverb naming the three greatest sorrows in man's lifetime: "To lie in bed and sleep not, to wait for someone who comes not, to try and please and please not." Well, I must have dozed at some point for I had disjointed dreams of dropping vital parts of the truck's engine into dark inaccessible recesses and getting my hands and arms trapped and wedged among the hard jagged crevasses.

Come morning, I brewed three cups of strong espresso, shared one with Mary, and then went out to face the dawn. I eagerly pulled the number one diesel injector. A black hole, the size of a large cigar, leered at me. I climbed up into the cab and shouted, "OK, sweetheart, I'll give it a go, and you let me know if any water comes out." She was perched atop the fender, her feet in the engine compartment, waiting expectantly. "Keep clear of the belts and fan," I cautioned. "Clunk," the engine said. "No water," she cheerfully reported. "I know," I murmured to myself. I lifted my lithe assistant out of the way, replaced the injector, and pulled number two. "Watch for the water, dearest." "I'm watching," she replied. I switched on the ignition, said a "Hail Mary," and winced at the heart-dropping familiar "clunk." Maybe I'd put the battery in backward or could I be out of diesel fuel? Two down and four to go. I was playing roulette with a six-cylinder diesel croupier. Time slipped by, and the routine was repeated. Number three was innocent. Numbers four and five reiterated the familiar maddening "clunk," and I was down to my last dollar. I unscrewed my last hope and tried, in a pleasant voice, asking, "Watch for water." "I'm watching," she replied, though I knew she was concerned for the pork roast she was preparing. "Cranking," I cautioned her. "Stand clear." I turned the key and with a growl and a roar and a shudder, the Old Girl turned over, ejecting a solid

LEE STATH (MARILEES)

stream of water out of the engine compartment and against a nearby tree. We both shouted for joy. "She blows!" I cried and clambered out of the cab to hold and be held as we watched the water seep from the guilty piston. It had taken us four hours; but we had, at last, isolated the problem. Now there was heavy, tedious, technical work to be done. "Let's take a break and see if the roast is ready for lunch. I'm weak from hunger," she confessed. Mary said to wash up, and we'd dine in half an hour.

With lunch out of the way, I scurried back to the cavernous interior of the opened hood. Lurking inside with its number six piston drained of all the intrusive water, I now had only to put a heavy socket wrench onto the scores of octagonal head bolts and pray. Remember that this sweetheart was of World War II vintage so there were no cumbersome air-conditioner units, blowers, computer casings, or other weird gadgets that prohibit entry in today's engines. I had ample room in which to crawl, scrunch up close, and begin the muscle work of breaking loose those untouched ancient bolts from their well-seated security. This was "man" work, and I bid my assistant mechanic to mount her ten-speed racing bike and pedal the eight kilometers to El Corte Ingles to shop for some special foods for tonight's banquet. I felt I would be under the hood, out of sight, and preoccupied with the head bolts for the rest of the day and would need no help.

I looked down our tree lined lane as she whizzed off on her own venture and then I snuggled up to my mistress and seated an eighteen-inch wrench, optimistically, on the first most accessible bolt. I leaned heavily on the end and gave it my all. The bolt grinned back. I replied with a few cautious hammer raps and braced my feet against the firewall and bent to the task. The bolt was proving to be a better man than I. Where was Mary? I needed an extension to increase the leverage. I unbent myself and wriggled out of the hood, scratched around my truck, and came back with a sturdy two-foot pipe. I reentered the tomb and dared this bolt to resist my science and strength. It was Archimedes who said, "Give me a long enough lever and a place to stand and I will move the earth." My ambitions were not of that magnitude, but my determination was a close second. With two hands and a greasy shoe, I applied myself with a steady pressure and was thrilled when I heard a "pop" and the wrench moved a few centimeters. Then a stab of fear tightened my already tight belly. Had I committed the "shade tree mechanic's" most feared offense? Had I snapped the bolt head off the bolt? I gingerly pressed back on a counterclockwise turn, and nothing fell off. The enemy was yielding; slowly, reluctantly loosening. I knew better then slack too much off at once. My well-worn manual had instructed, step by step, which bolt was to be loosened next and at what position it occupied among those twenty-four unrelenting protuberances. I cautiously followed those instructions and I promise not to elucidate the variety of challenges each bolt produced, but it was amazing the different characters each one possessed. The hours were interspersed with dropped pipes, wrenches, sockets, and rags. Each time, I cried out for Mary. "Where is that damn woman when I need her?" Ah, yes, I sent her shopping. Nothing she could do here to help. I cursed myself each time I fumbled and dropped something. If it fell to the ground, it meant reliving the painful ordeal of uncurling my body and extricating

LEE STATH (MARILEES)

myself from that unsymmetrical prison to climb down and crawl under the truck to retrieve the elusive piece. That was frustrating, time-consuming, and exhausting. But worse were the times when the object did not fall under the truck. It was when I heard it ping-ponging like a ball in a pinball machine, and after the familiar ground search proved fruitless, then began the hunt amid the countless recesses of an engine where a small thingy could hide. "Mary, where the hell are you?" With the repeated clamoring in and out and the tussle with each bolt, my strength was ebbing; still, I was gaining. When Mary returned, four hours later, both

saddle bags crammed with food, I had lost my anger. I was too exhausted to say anything other than, "Hello, sweetheart. I'm almost done here. Let's call it a day." And so ended the first half of the battle.

"I remember this sunset was sweet."

Blessed with another glorious sunrise over the Mediterranean, I was loathed to climb back into my greasy coveralls; but there was dirty, greasy, heavy work awaiting us. I was elated over having removed all the cylinder head bolts without incident. I knew the nontechnical job of lifting the 75-pound solid, cast-iron head straight up off the engine block and out of the way was going to require some technical ingenuity. As fate would dictate, the lush eucalyptus trees, under which we had chosen to park, not only afforded us cool shade but almost directly over our ailing engine was a limb sturdy enough to support the weight I planned to hang on it. I was going to send Mary up the tree, but I wasn't too confident of her knot-tying so I scrambled up while Mary laid out the block and tackle. Thanks to our profession, we had an abundance of cables and pulleys. Once up in the tree, I was struck at how far I could see. The sandy beach was only a few hundred meters from our camp site; and farther out, in that deep aqua marine blue of the Med, white sailboats were in a regatta. Life was going on all around us with not a care in the world. It was so tranquil and soothing I could only reply, "Just now, my dear," when Mary shouted angrily, "Well, are you going to pull this up or not?" I hoisted the pulleys and rope and made fast to the smooth limb on which I sat. Back to earth, I attached the tackle to the lifting ring that I had screwed into the cylinder head. There was a moment of silence and then I asked "Are you ready, woman?" And we put our weight onto this triple double pulley and eased that puppy up and off the block so smoothly we could only rejoice and wonder what we had done right. I was proud of Mary. She had really put her back into it. The time was noon, and the sun was hot. We were both lathered in sweat, but I felt the hard part was done. Next the new gasket, reverse the procedure, reset the valves, a little timing adjustment, and our mobile home would be mobile again. But that could wait until tomorrow. After all, this was Spain. The sea was near. We were hot, happy, and into our swimsuits without a care. We had become a part of this "Land of Manana."

LEE STATH (MARILEES)

## Chapter LXXV

# The End Is Near

WE EAGERLY ACCEPTED the happy chore of another season with Knie in Switzerland. It was now 1979, and these faithful kids had stuck it out for ten long years. Could I keep them satisfied or hoodwinked another year? No easy task. Understandably, they were suspicious; and Graeme, along with Trevor, had long planned their own act. They had even gone so far as building their own net (seemingly a vital step to making a new act). I had made it a practice, as Mary had taught me, to keep our contract details strictly private. Many acts would boast of their contracts and the inflated salaries they claimed to be earning. What we signed for was known only to Mary and I. Yet before I signed a new contract, I would approach our group and ask if they were agreeable to the new terms I presented; if so, I would sign.

In the midst of our engagement, Trevor came into our truck and said he had something important to tell me. Mary made tea. We sat; and he told me, haltingly, that he and Graeme had intercepted a letter of mine, steamed it open, and read the contents. It was our contract with the Italian Circus for the 1980 season. This had festered within him for some weeks, and now he needed to purge himself. I was overcome not with the confession but with his honesty and integrity. To come forth with such an admission was staggering. I could only express my admiration at such character. The contract, incidentally, was as I had proposed to them and I too was exonerated.

But it wasn't all over for me. There were still moments of glory and success to be had. It was now the year of 1981, and I had had these South African kids in my care for twelve years. It's rare that a big act as ours, six individuals, can survive in the circus world so long; what with the infighting, outside agitation, competition, and jealousy. A family act manages because it's family. I've always said, a circus act is like a marriage but without the sex. So with those many years of being together, day in and day out, I finally succumbed to the struggle. I gathered the clan together and told them, come season's end, it was all over. We could go our separate ways. The constant squabbling and dissension had taken its toll. They could have the rigging, as previously agreed, and try it on their own. It was time to terminate the Marilee Flyers.

LEE STATH (MARILEES)

# Chapter LXXVI

# Just Call Me Maestro

W ITH THE BREAKUP, fate, or "Lee luck," intervened once again. We were in Italy on the "American Circus." (How many "American" circuses had we worked on outside America?) Three brothers, the Tognis, owned this particular one. Each brother had two siblings' and every year, when they hired a new flying act to join their show, all six of the children were put under the tutorage of the new act and ordered, "Learn to fly," but never with any success. Suddenly, I had those six young fledglings and the order was "Teach them to fly." In all truth, I must have been there at just the right moment. Six of the most handsome and beautiful athletes (four boys and two girls) I had not seen collectively. I was old and tired. They were young, eager, and spoiled. Children of the circus owners, they were unaccustomed to critical or harsh orders. I gave them both.

I will not retell the grueling scenario of training a new flying troupe. This was a bit different since they were all circus kids. They had been in and around circus acts since diaper days. In short, they were already circus artists. All I had to do was teach them to fly. Better term still was "force" them to fly. Once the novelty wore off, it became a battle of wills. Director's children are not used to working when they do not want to. A firm hand was foreign but necessary. I had been given carte blanche to shape them into flyers, and for the first time, they were driven to work and practice until I was satisfied. Marco, one of the more talented in the group, came in for practice after the last show; and I detected a hint of alcohol. Italian pasta, salad, and a bit of wine, it was probably the norm. But I pointed an accusing finger at him and said he was not going up on my rigging to practice with that offense. He could sit in the seats and watch. He ambled off, muttering in Italian something like, "Big deal. All I've got to do is get drunk, and

I'm excused from this madman's madness." But with this kind of unfamiliar discipline, we were very shortly offering an acceptable flying act.

Now we were the "Togni-Marilee Flyers." The family was

"Togni-Marilee Flyers."

bursting with pride over their children's success. Still it was somewhat disconcerting, during the act, to have all three fathers running under the net, shouting encouragement and warnings each time one of their cherished offspring went for a trick. In spite of this, the act was a success.

My mission was accomplished, and it didn't go unappreciated. They were lavish with their gifts and praise. On opening night in Rome, I was surprised and a bit resentful at the added pressure when, near the end of the act, they announced that Marco would attempt to be the first

Italian man to catch a triple. I was tense with the added pressure, but Marco seemed cool and almost indifferent. We caught the trick. Actually, I caught the trick, and the crowd responded with a roar of appreciation. This was indeed a momentous occasion for the Togni Circus. A grand celebration was held in a reserved restaurant. I was a hero in their eyes. I had taken their unruly, undisciplined children and transformed them into a first-class flying trapeze act.

The most gratifying treasure I received from the Togni family was the gift "Nono," the old grandfather, gave to me. I had completed the matinee; and as I unwrapped my wristbands, just outside the tent, Nono, the aged patriarch sitting in the sun, called out, "Ehi, Marilees, veni qui." I obliged and went to him where he took both my hands into his thin frail hands and shook them both and in a hoarse whisper spoke two words that were gifts of jewels to me. "El maestro! El maestro," he said it twice with deep emotion. The old circus gentleman called me "Maestro," and he really meant maestro. It was time to quit, time to leave. I had achieved all that the wonderful world of circus could give me.

The words of John Dryden express my feelings completely.

"Happy the man, and happy he alone.
He who can call today his own-
He who, secure within, can say:
    "Tomorrow do thy worst, for I have lived today!
Be fair or foul, or rain or shine,
The joys I have possessed, in spite of fate are mine,
Nor heaven itself over the past has power;
But what has been, has been; and I have had my hour!"

# Chapter LXXVII

# The Price of Success

PARIS, APRIL 27, 2008
Long, tiring flight with Delta across the Atlantic. We Landed at Charles de Gaulle and with my diminished French managed to move my fatigued Mary and self to the Gare du Nord. Struggled to bribe a taxi for the short haul to our old first love of a hotel, the Blanche Fontaine, in Montmartre. How fifty-one years had changed it. It was nothing like the castle we had entered on our first conquest of France. I had booked us in for four nights, via the Internet, and dammed the cost. With the dollar down to almost two to one Euro, I swallowed the cost of $1,000 and tried not to remember the $17 I paid per week back in 1957. The man who said, "You can never go home," must have seen me making these grandiose plans. Then too, Mary was not the same woman. I left her in the now dreary lounge. She was exhausted, near tears, and swearing she was not able to climb another stair. I believed her. This once fit athlete had become an old crippled woman. The beauty that was always a part of her through so many years was now dulled and masked. It trailed behind in all those seasons of brutal work and physical abuse. She strove to keep that damned circus banner, "The show must go on," aloft and high. How

dearly she now paid for those eighty years of effort and dedication. The sleepless nights when I tried gentle massage and tender words to ease the pain that throbbed in her arthritic broken vertebra, her aching shoulders. One aspirin and the infrequent cortisone shot was the only concession to drugs she would tolerate.

Seated in the lounge, both knees swollen and offering little support, I tried to console her, pointing out," Look, my sweet, we've come back home. Rest here just a moment, and I'll run these two bags (we had finally learned to travel light) up to our room. Then when you're ready, we'll make the final attack on those few remaining stairs, and you'll have your own bed to rest in." "No, Lee! Don't leave me. I know you're not coming back." This was a growing fear, a near obsession, that I would leave and she would be alone. This once resilient woman had allowed me to take over and provide all her needs. Reluctantly and resentfully, she had lost her battle of independence; and I was, saddly, her protector and guardian. She dozed for a moment, and I made the run to our room with our bags. I didn't allow myself the time to acknowledge or ask, "Where was the room we entered so many years ago?" I only parted the curtains and pried open a window, but where was that breath-stealing view of those French garrets, rows of chimneys, open courtyard, trees, flowers, and shrubs? What were those tall sterile apartment buildings doing outside our window? No time for tears. I hurried down for my Mary and eased her slowly, oh so slowly, down those broad wide set steps and finally up to our room in Paris. A dream realized? We had four weeks to endure.

Four long weeks? After fifty-five years of marriage, together twenty-four hours a day, one wonders how a relationship under such stress could survive. In our case, we stayed together not for the children's sake (we were blessed and had none); it was the act that held us together. How many times, when things went wrong in the air or elsewhere, and the tension and anger were palpable, one would spit out, "When this contract is finished, so am I. I'm out of here." Thank, God, we always made up, and the show did go on.

LEE STATH (MARILEES)

# Chapter LXXVIII

# The Korean Curse

MORNING IN PARIS came, and I was pleased that we had both slept well. It was quite a relief since Mary had been coughing continually throughout the night back home. We were concerned over the wisdom of undertaking this month long trip if she was really sick. I brought tablets and cough syrup along, hoping it would not worsen. These week-long coughing spells came once or twice every winter and spring, and it all dated back to a three-week engagement we had in Korea just south of the Thirty-eighth Parallel. We were at one of the army bases to entertain, and it was bitter cold. Up we went, every night, in skimpy leotards and Mary in her warmest bikini. That was tough on us all. But the hotel in which they had us quartered had no central heating. Instead, a large earthen urn was brought ceremoniously into our cramped room, and a glowing charcoal fire

"It's nice and warm; just don't breathe."

radiated some warmth. We huddled around it until fatigue forced us into bed.

We clung to each other throughout the night, and why we were not asphyxiated, I don't know. But Mary's cough started then, and it had a permanent damaging effect on her lungs. Even the distant "KRUMP-KRUMP" of shells exploding sporadically had little effect on our already-diminished morale. God bless our troops and thank you Jesus for payday.

LEE STATH (MARILEES)

# Chapter LXXIX

# We'll Always Have Paris

**B**UT NOW BACK in Paris, with peace and time to kill, I thought it would be entertaining to take the Metro out to Filles du Calvaire and see if the old Cirque d'hiver was working. We didn't expect to find any old friends or someone who might remember us, but there might be some aerial act of worth, or better yet, a really bad aerial act at which we could snicker and belittle over a glass of wine and compare with our glory days. That would have been fun; but it was bad timing since the circus was closed and gone out on the road, putting up the tent and riggings, doing two shows, staying for two days and then off to the next town to do it all over again: ad infinitum. There was no envy or nostalgia for that on my part, reminding me of the joke where the stable worker is shoveling loads of exotic animal shit in a pile to be loaded on the wagon. All the while, with every shovel full, he is cursing and moaning about the disgusting monotonous work. When his coworker finally asks, "Hell, man, why don't you quit?" "What," the astonished complainer replies, "and give up showbiz?"

So with this attitude, we went next door to the corner bar where I had a cognac and Mary sipped a glass of vin rouge. The place was empty; and as we sat there, the lone patrons in the early afternoon, my memory slipped back some many years when we first visited this dinky bistro, the Café des Artists. It was in here that I had my first boeuf Bourguignon. To this point, it is the finest food I have eaten in France. Beef so rich, so tender, so colorful, a dark red, more maroon and vegetables melded together for many patient hours. All this, a crisp baguette of bread and a cheap wine proved to be an unexpected surprise and pleasure.

More surprising and even more gratifying was when the bartender refilled our glasses, and in reply to my quizzical look, he nodded at the unshaven man standing behind us. This working-class gentleman approached, pardoned himself with genuine humility for having intruded, and said, "You are the Marilees, yes?" It had been a few years since we had played in Paris; so, somewhat surprised, I answered, "Yes, we are." Then he paid me, us, our greatest compliment. He said he remembered seeing us work, here in Paris, some years ago and he declared it was the finest flying act he had seen; and, being a working circus man, he had seen many. "Madam was formidable. I've never seen such beauty combined with such artistry and ability. I kiss your hand." And he did. But that was so cool. To be picked out in an empty room, in a foreign country, and being recognized after those years made me feel like a celebrity. If only he had asked for my autograph. Of course, I knew it was Mary's beauty and ability of which he spoke, me being a lowly "spear carrier" on stage; but I bask in that warm, pleasant glow I experienced in that cold French café even now.

That didn't happen often. Unless you count the time we were in New York to see the Russian State Circus. As expected, they had produced and sent out the best acts to be gathered in their country. It was late as we left the show, mingling among the hundreds of other patrons. Suddenly, two well-dressed women rushed over to Mary, who was swaddled in her full-length mink coat and gushed over how great the show was and in particular how sensational Mary had been. Mary was cool and aloof and said, in broken English, "I, and my comrades, thank you." She swirled around, leaving two very impressed old ladies. She never considered destroying the illusion that we were great Russian artists with the fact that we too were only spectators. I guess one cannot hide one's talents under a bushel basket or a mink coat.

Now it was day three. We had long ago seen both left and right banks of the River Seine. We had climbed the endless worn steps to the top of Notre Dame. There I clowned around, doing my Quasimodo impersonation among the silent ancient gargoyles to the consternation of a few tourists. We canvassed both sides, repeatedly, of the Champs Elyse; up the Tour Eifel (we took the elevator this time) where I was reminded again of the terrifying fear where acrophobia can numb all logical reason of heights. It was over the edge of this tower that a film was shot of Rose Gould performing her trapeze act so many years ago, but it was all so clear and frightening still. I clung to the elevator rails and implored Mary not to go toward the edge. She laughed and asked me not to act like a little girl. But then I couldn't understand her fear of elevators and closed spaces. Down from the dizzying heights of the famous tower and I was reminded when we were guests at the Olympia Theater where our old friend, Larry Griswold, was performing his show-stopping comedy trampoline act, and on the same bill, one of the last few performances of the legendary Edith Piaf. What a privilege. After the show, after midnight, we were out on the town, always a different restaurant with hours of eating, drinking, and reliving our performances and audience reactions. There were both failures and triumphs, but with friends, other artists speaking the language of "showbiz." Oh, those were halcyon days.

How about the Louvre? We had wandered for hours, no, days through that maze of masterpieces. Back when the Mona Lisa was within touch and only a sleepy old guard, sitting nearby, asking us not to. That was a lifetime ago, and now we had returned with no desire to do it again. We were victims of Weltsmertzen, ennui, and abused worn-out bodies. So I sit in our room past two and three in the morning. Unable to sleep and counting, not sheep, but how many more days must we sleep till noon, amble down to the corner for an espresso double and quasaint? (Really, the highpoint of the day.) Then we would meander the streets, sit at the sidewalk cafes, and watch the people go by. I must confess that it was fascinating, such a kaleidoscope of humanity. I grew weary pointing at the ceaseless stream of lithe, athletic, slender humans. But there they went. Endless bunches of bicycles, small Vespa scooters with two astride; tiny two-seated cars whizzing in a dizzying pattern among all these slender people. Now a dozen single line skaters zip in among the melee, while an occasional lone jogger wends through the city crowd. This is our new way of seeing Paris. In years gone by, we were part of it.

LEE STATH (MARILEES)

# Chapter LXXX

# Marriage, Again and Again

I'M TIRED OF drinking cognac and eating pomme frites. Just one more day, April 28, our fifty-fifth wedding anniversary. I say it's our fifty-fifth, but it could be more or less. We were working on the Clyde Beatty Circus in San Diego back in 1953. After the night show, a bunch of the other performers joined us, and we crossed the border into Tijuana. That too was a different Mexico half a century ago. We ate, danced, drank mucho tequila, and, after some good-natured prodding, decided to get married. There was a small room next to the bar; and with half a dozen words in Mexican, fifty pesos, and a slip of paper with our names, date, and a large legal-looking stamp, we were married; I think. More tequila and we were back to the circus to consummate the marriage, again. I never felt good about that (the Mexican marriage, I mean). So a year later, on April 28, 1954, in San Antonio, we did it again (the

"And a good time was had by all."

marriage I mean) at a justice of the peace. That seemed pretty binding to me. Yet in Vienna, Austria, Mary got it arranged by our friend, Pater Schoenig, the circus priest, to have us married by the monsignor in the awesome gothic cathedral in the center of Vienna. A Catholic wedding and now Mary was at peace. The third time, for her, was a charm.

LEE STATH (MARILEES)

# Chapter LXXXI

# Forgetting Paris

I WANTED SO HARD for this anniversary, this breakaway from the sad monotonous existence Mary seems bound to in our Texas home, to be a joyous rebirth. But today our anniversary was taken up walking a few blocks for coffee, sitting curbside, and sipping wine; and even the weather has turned colder, eliminating my idea of taking the little motorized tourist train up to the Sacre Coure. It was a bit windy and chilly in the open coaches, so we found another café and watched the throngs of tourists troop by, photographing and filming every building in sight. I can recall, it was not so long ago, when we raced up those steps and hooted derisively at the old lame and lazy tourists who took the little train. Now we couldn't even do that.

Back to the hotel room where I once again rechecked our planned itinerary, train departures, reservations, train numbers, and seat numbers. It all matched. It should all work out. It should all be simple. I had never before been so farsighted and efficient. All the previous years, we had just set out and took what we could find. That meant sleeping in our car on several occasions, but now it looked promising, and all it took was a little more money.

My sweet delicate mate slept a few hours, but her cough has returned. So as we returned to the streets, I visited a pharmacy for another cough depressant. Reading the directions, it stressed on seeing one's doctor if the cough persisted. That's still a month away. I'm hoping the weeks in Spain will bring back her spirit and strength. At one of the cafes, I asked the French waiter if he could heat a glass of wine for her. He returned with a metal-caged glass of hot red wine, half a lemon, and a shaker of cinnamon powder. It helped her at once; and his considerateness dispelled, for me, all those stories of rude, arrogant French waiters

A brief synopsis of what transpired since our fifty-fifth anniversary celebration. We checked out of the old hotel, taxied to the train station, and managed to board the right train, find the right coach, and even the correct reserved seats. The train was swift, and the scenery was a blur till we were in Zurich at the Hauptbahnhof, which left us only a few blocks to our reserved room at the Hotel Wahalla. I carried our small suitcases very slowly as Mary seemed only able to walk a few paces, needing to stop for minutes, complaining of fatigue, shortness of breath, and cursing the doctors who had pressed her into the triple bypass heart surgery that had changed her life and mine.

It was such a joy, at the hotel, to be able to communicate in German. We were warmly greeted. I exchanged some dollars for Swiss francs; and we found the room on the fifth floor to be an enchanting garret, the sort of place one might imagine a promising painter or writer might have chosen. There was modern plumbing and the convenience of an elevator, but we had to take precautions and stoop down, crossing from bathroom to bedroom, as the heavy wooden support beams ran dangerously low along the sloping ceiling. Once settled, we were eager for some well-remembered Swiss cuisine. Just on the corner was the typical Gasthaus and things had not much changed. Even the freedom to smoke made it difficult to find a corner, in which to cringe, seeking some sanctuary. The food was terrible. Nothing on the menu resembled the exquisite platters of twenty years previous, a dry flat Wienerschnitzel that could have come from MacDonald's. Nevertheless, the beer was good, and the friendly waitress understood my plea for some hot red wine for Mary and brought the proper Gluhwine she needed. She slept well.

Another evening of dried veal, beer, and wine. We returned to our garret and prepared for our train departure and a rush to Spain. Well, maybe not a rush. We had a few stops to make: Genève, Montpellier, customs at the border, and finally into Spain. Now the fun could begin.

## Chapter LXXXII

# Sadness In The Sun

THE TRAIN INTO Spain was a little less grand than the previous Euro rail travels, particularly the passage from Paris to Berlin a few years earlier when we slipped silently through the scenic countryside. I was mystified as we paralleled the German autobahn and saw new BMWs and Mercedes seemingly gliding backward. I queried the conductor as to their reduced speed. "No, no," he explained, "they're probably revving at 160 to 180 kilometers per hour. The illusion is created by our speed of 300 kilometers per hour. So relax and watch them disappear." We were racing along the rails at 180 to 200 miles an hour. Berlin was not far away, not so on the RENFE line. We didn't dawdle and we were in no rush, but the pace and luxury were not the same. Yet we arrived on time at Estacio de Franca, the station in Barcelona, where a taxi had no trouble finding our hotel on the Via Ramblas.

I had booked the hotel El Calderon on the Internet and expected the worse. But even Mary, my watermark, was impressed. Not the same experience of a few years earlier when we entered the city unannounced and no prior booking. It was past midnight; and as we sat at an outdoor café, phoning, I was rejected time after time, searching for a lodging for the night. It seemed there was no room at the inn. I hailed a taxi and asked his aid. The problem, it turned out, was the Spanish Grand Prix took place that weekend, and all hotels were booked. Mary sipped some vino tinto, while the taxi driver called endlessly around town, seeking a room. After his many efforts, he said the only available place was some eighteen kilometers out of town. I reconciled myself to spending the night at the outdoor café or in the lobby of one of the nearby hotels. I thanked the taxi for his gracious efforts and time spent, but he would accept no gratuity for all he had done on our behalf. One thirty now, and the bar closed at three. I told Mary to be patient, and I circled the block in desperation. A large hotel stood around the corner. I entered and asked the desk clerk for a room. He shocked me by asking for how many nights. "Just two would be fine." "You are fortunate, indeed," he replied. "We have one cancellation. It will be 350 Euro per night." *Great Scott*, I thought. That's over $400 a night. "Fine, I'll bring my wife right in." A Spaniard, Alonso, won the grand prix race.

# Chapter LXXXIII

# Home At Last

THAT WAS SOME years earlier. Now we were in our reserved suite where we rested, ate, and drank but found little more to do. I felt we should revisit the Sagrada Familia Cathedral, still under construction after more than one hundred years. It was Antoni Gaudi i Cornet who first envisioned this masterpiece of flowering fantasy.

"The Sagrada familia in Barcelona."

I wanted to see what progress had been made since we first stumbled upon it so many years before. But Mary's physical decline could not allow it. Before we moved on, I coaxed her down to the Ramblas among the surging, joyous crowds; and she seemed to enjoy that, but she kept repeating that the vacation would begin when we got down to Spain. "But, sweetheart, this is Barcelona. We are in Spain." "I mean Javea. That's where Spain begins," she countered. I knew what she meant. That was the little fishing village we had discovered so long ago on our first visit in 1960. It was our home for a while but had changed, even before we left it. But there was the Hotel Patilla. Maybe that would renew her old memories and our vacation could begin.

"The massif of Montgo on the Costa Blanca."

I pressed on; and at the sight of Montgo, that massive mount perched on the edge of the sea, I shouted, "Look, sweetheart, we're almost there." Bypassing Denia, we were soon on old familiar streets and down to the waterfront. The road to our old camping grounds was torn up and impassable. We drove through the town, and I asked, "How about the hotel by the bay? You always liked that." But no, we drove on through Javea and never even turned off the engine.

I should have suspected something then. I drove aimlessly on, heading for the Costa del Sol, maybe a new part of Spain. We idled, slowly, through Malaga, Torremolinos, Marbella; and if one didn't know better, you would believe you were in Miami. No pause, only a restless night at a Spanish version of Motel 6. The morning broke clear and sun-filled as it can only do in southern Spain. Mary lay close beside me, crying softly and sobbed, "I want to go home."

# Chapter LXXXIV

# The Ultimate Betrayal

SO FINALLY WE are in our house. We have, surprisingly, been here twenty-two years. Yet I know she doesn't call it home. It was only last night. She asked me to come to bed early and read to her. Lying close to each other as I read her to sleep was, she always said, the best part of the day.

Only a short while and she turned over, away from the light, and let out such a deep mournful sigh. I closed our book and called for help. In a moment, they came and took my Mary away. A massive stroke, they explained. Left side of the

"The best part of the day."

brain, I believe. I got to hold her once again, and I breathed in her ear, "I love you, Mary." She gripped me fiercely and whispered, I'm not certain, but it was either "I want to go home" or "I'm going home."

"Goodnight, sweet princess."

Mary Rose Stath

No services planned

Kerrville – Mary Rose (nee Atterbury) Stath, world-renowned trapeze artist born in a circus wagon somewhere in Nebraska in the year of either 1924, 1922 or 1917 and a member of the Flying Marilees, gave her last performance on October 13, 2013, at the age of 95, but missed the big trick and went on to meet "The Big Catcher in the Sky".

# Glossary (She Flies Through The Air)

Apc-
World War II euphemism meaning an All Purpose Capsule.

Art Concello-
Outstanding flyer of the 30s and later general manager of Ringling Brothers Circus.

Back yard-
Back end of a circus tent where artists and animals gather for their entrance. Also their place of meeting and gossiping.

Barker-
Man on a sideshow front whose job is to talk customers into the show.

Boffo-
Big success

Botas-
Spanish: goat or animal skin bag used to hold wine

Brudershaft-
German: Brotherhood. Drinking toast to seal the relationship.

Candy butchers-
Circus salesmen dispensing popcorn and other refreshments.

| | |
|---|---|
| Carnies- | Anyone associated with or working for a carnival |
| Cherry pie- | The after show chores of cleaning up for extra money. |
| Churros- | Spanish: long sticks of pastry, deep fried and sugar coated. |
| Donniker- | Circus term for toilets. Early English origin where knickers is the word for underpants. In the days of outdoor facilities one might say, "I'm going outside to *down me knickers.*" corrupted to *down knickers* or *donniker.* |
| Dorp- | Afrikaans: Small village or town. |
| First of may- | Circus name for any new comer. A greenhorn. |
| folks boat- | Scandinavian built boat of clinker or lap strake construction. |
| Gasthaus- | German: Guest house. An inn |
| Gigante- | Spanish: Giant. Any of a costumed or stilt walking ogre seen at all fiestas. |
| Gilley- | Circus form of transport to and from the circus grounds. |

LEE STATH (MARILEES)

| | |
|---|---|
| Hausfrau- | German: house keeper or dowdy woman. |
| Hoch- | German: high or ultra |
| Jungled- | The act of being close or living in confined quarters. |
| Joints- | Stalls on a carnival. |
| Le Petomane- | See "google" for description. |
| Kafir- | Afrikaans: common name for a native or black. |
| Kinkers- | Circus acrobats. |
| Macht nicht- | German: It doesn't matter. |
| Mensch- | German: People or mankind. Figuratively an exclamation "Wow" |
| Milking- | Theatrical term. Pleading for extra applause |
| Nicht wahr?- | German: "Isn't that true?" |
| Nut- | The total expense required to operate a show. |
| Ou' est mon trou?- | French: "Where is my hole?" |

over inflate- Danger of early diving suit's the result of excess air ballooning the diver to the surface.

Parador- Spanish: An ancient monastery or castle converted into a modern, luxury inn or hotel.

Patch- The legal man on a show whose job is to right any unlawful or questionable acts.

Penny pitch- A small concession on a carnival. A game of chance involving tossing pennies onto a small target.

Perks- extra benefits

Pie car- A circus wagon used exclusively for snacks, drinks and gambling.

Possum belly- A locker or storage bin under a truck.

Quasaint- French: A French pastry.

Salted- Theatrical ploy of seating paid customers to loudly support an act.

saltomortal- German: an aerial somersault.

LEE STATH (MARILEES)

| | |
|---|---|
| Spec- | Circus spectacular. Large extravaganza of the entire circus used to introduce or close the show. |
| Straw house- | A sold out show where additional seating is afforded by spreading straw on the ground. |
| Swabies- | navy slang for any sailor. |
| Tamiami Trail- | The main highway running from Tampa to Miami. |
| Towners- | Term used by show people for the customers or locals from the town. |
| Two or more- | Ploy used by circus owners that requires an act to do a second number or some times a third in order to procure a booking. |
| Web- | A one inch diameter cotton rope combed loose and then pulled through an inch diameter cotton tube. |
| Web broads- | Young female aerialists who perform simple acrobatic tricks on a web |
| Web sitter- | The man or worker who assists the web broad by holding, slacking and spinning the web as required. |

Weisithit-       Carnival language meaning "with it" or
                 one of us.

Weltsmerzen-     German: world pain, weary, ennui

Wirt-            German: Tavern owner or inn keeper

LEE STATH (MARILEES)